Integration and the Support Service
Changing Roles in Special Education

Integration and the Support Service
Changing Roles in Special Education

Peter Clough
Geoff Lindsay

NFER-NELSON

Published by The NFER-NELSON Publishing Company Ltd,
Darville House, 2 Oxford Road East,
Windsor, Berkshire SL4 1DF, UK

First published 1991
© 1991 Peter Clough and Geoff Lindsay

British Library Cataloguing in Publication Data
Lindsay, Geoff
    Integration and the support service: changing roles in special education.
    I. Title   II. Clough, Peter
    371.9
    ISBN 0 7005 1266 7

Phototypeset by David John Services Ltd, Maidenhead, Berks.
Printed by Billing & Sons Ltd., Worcester

ISBN 0 7005 1266 7
Code 8507 02 4

Contents

List of Tables and Figures

Preface

The 1981 Education Act set a course for the education of children with special educational needs (SEN) in the UK; they were to be brought as far as possible into the mainstream of educational provision. Critics of the Act have pointed out that the legislation allowed for wide margins of interpretation of this mandate, but for all that there is not an LEA that has not been affected in some degree by this statutory drive to integration.

The changes which the Act called for – if not demanded – have been felt throughout schools and LEAs, and the central principle of reorganization is that of support; support for learners so that they can participate in the curriculum without distinction from their peers; and support for teachers so that their teaching is differentiated for process rather than goal.

Where the changes have been remarkable, a great deal of the necessary support has come from within schools; the disbanding of 'remedial' classes and 'remedial' teachers has most often led to the setting up of in-class support systems with limited withdrawal of pupils, frequently within 'whole-school SEN policies'. In these systems, teachers who might previously have attended withdrawn groups of remedial pupils now make up their timetable supporting those individuals as they follow a 'normal' curriculum. 'Support' is also sometimes offered to subject teachers variously in the appropriate preparation of their teaching material, in its actual delivery to the class as a whole and in the evaluation of its outcomes.

This book is concerned with the mostly parallel changes that are taking place within the broader systems of support at LEA level; the ways in which LEAs organize their support services for schools and their staffs. In particular, the book addresses the issues facing LEAs with a typical array of special educational needs, and an array of support services traditionally designed to meet them. The book seeks to understand these issues, needs and services as they are redefined by a new legislative context – that of the 1988 Education Reform Act.

Acknowledgements

The study reported in this book was carried out over some two and a half years, and involved a large number of people. We are grateful to all the people we talked to from City LEA; its elected members, officers and advisory and – most of all – teaching staffs; although necessarily anonymous here, they will no doubt know themselves! The principal fieldworkers who contributed directly to the preparation of the evaluation reports were Veronica Wigley, Paul Geldeart and Andrew Wallwork and their work substantially informs a number of these chapters. Other contributions to the work reported here were made by Dave Melbourne, Ernie Shackleton and Liz Udloff; Val Stokes was a wonderful secretary to the project, and Michele Biggin generously helped with the typing of the final drafts.

Chapter 1
The Supportive Principle

'Support' is now a commonplace term in providing for learners with special educational needs (SEN): support for both pupils and their teachers by staff from within and without the school. The principle behind supportive structures established at school and local education authority (LEA) levels is that, whatever their difficulties, all learners should participate as far as possible in the mainstream of 'ordinary' school culture and curricula; this is their entitlement, and supportive education is about organizing help appropriate to the special needs of those learners and, indeed, appropriate to the needs of their 'regular' teachers. In this sense, the supportive principle calls for the removal of all sorts of barriers to education in the classroom and the school – instead of removing the children themselvs.

In this book we are specifically concerned with the role within this broad initiative of the support service, and this chapter considers how such a service can develop an accountable structure for working with schools that is responsive to particular school needs, and yet provocative of new developments. It discusses some of the difficulties that face these innovations, tracing those difficulties to the traditions of practice that have determined current organization, and highlighting the ideology of the 1981 Education Act (GB.DES, 1981) as a new principle of organization.

Constructions of Special Educational Need

How do support teachers and services know what to do when they go into school? How do they know what the school wants? How do they set about delivering what is wanted, particularly if it is not in their immediate repertoire? How do they know if what they have done is acceptable? How do they know what to do next?

Behind every decision made in response to a special educational need, there lie traditions of practice that more or less evidently affect the processes and outcomes of that action. How the individual teacher, the department, the school and the LEA *construct* and respond to a problem situation is determined by the habits of interpretation characteristic to each of them at their different levels in the overall structure. The sum of these constructions of SEN – whether they operate at the individual or the LEA level – makes up a particular special educational needs community.

This is also a community with wide and diverse views on what SEN are, and on how they should be dealt with, and not all these views are made explicit as statements. They are more likely to be inferred from particular organizational structures: this LEA has closed all its special schools, while that one is actually still building them; this school has a rigidly structured remedial department, while that one has a subject-based learning resource team, and so on. But in each case, and at every level, these responses to difficulty or disability express, if only implicitly, a particular construction of special educational needs.

For a support service, this range of interpretations may make an equally broad range of demands on its resources; different schools may want different things from the service, according to the dominant construction of special educational needs within the school. How the school sees its problems and needs, and how it has typically been organized to meet them in the past will condition the demands made on an external support service.

However, the support service itself operates as an equally important conditioner of the school's demand. In the interaction between the school and the support service, the school is constrained in the demand it makes not only by its own construction of the problems, but by what it perceives as being on offer from the service; and in the same way the service is limited both by its own resources and by the degrees of flexiblity it perceives in the school. To a large extent, what the support teacher decides to do will be determined by traditions of practice that in turn quickly suggest a course of action. The teacher's own experience and the school's familiar system collude – often inexplicitly – to select a technique from a range of possibilities. In this way the school and the support service find themselves in a potentially dynamic interaction attempting to match resource to demand within the limits of their perceived established practice.

But this dynamism is often only potential; for the action a support service can take arises from a repertoire of habitual contact with the school. More frequently, the habitual interactions between the school and the support service serve to delimit the options open in any given instance; thus a school that has typically used its fortnightly visiting support teacher in one particular way – say, for intensive reading work with whichever child appeared to need it at that time – is, in the normal run of things, unlikely to ask for anything else, nor is the support teacher very likely to offer other alternatives. In this way a mutually validating and often harmonious practice becomes a tradition.

In the old dispensation, remedial departments and support services were made for each other in this rather obvious way. The prevalent construction of learning difficulty that they shared saw a deficit in the child as the organizing principle of their relationship. This construction concentrated largely on reading difficulty as the source of school failure, and saw *remedial* action on the child – rather than on his or her environment – as the only appropriate solution. Thus problems became largely technical ones, in the sense that they called for special techniques (which were readily, if unwittingly, legitimated by educational psychological services – themselves effectively organized by a theory of child-deficit) (Clough, 1988).

This easy characterization of a learning difficulty being independent of its learning context thus created a technical solution for specific problems; for the problems come as it were with their solution implicit, or at least with some outline or guarantee of a remedial response already implicit in their diagnosis. We take for granted that technical solutions are available for technically identified problems; it is ultimately a question of running through the repertoire until the appropriate one is found. And in this way the system of referral characteristic of special education is created, as children appear to call for ever more specialized techniques. Thus Dessent has written:

Whatever else education involves it is first and foremost an administrative and organisational system whereby one group of professionals are invested with responsibility for handicapped and 'difficult-to-teach' children. At the same time other groups are absolved from such responsibility. Special education has come to

> be described and justified . . . in terms of its small teaching groups, special curricula, expertise and methods, but its historical roots lie in the need to remove responsibility for teaching children with special needs from class teachers in normal schools. (Dessent, 1983, p. 90)

Remedial support services have in the past played an important role in this process, often validating through their support the tendency of schools to separate their 'difficult-to-teach' children.

As is well documented elsewhere (see Gross and Gipps, 1987; Moses *et al.*, 1988; etc.), this situation changed greatly, often radically, over the 1980s, and has done so increasingly as 'new' constructions of special educational need have emerged in keeping with the spirit of the 1981 legislation. At the centre of the Act is a view of SEN as *relative* phenomena – specific *events* tied to particular learning environments rather than enduring *conditions* reflecting stable abilities and disabilities. The perceived source of difficulty is moved outside of the learner's head, as it were, to his or her learning environment; while action on those difficulties moves correspondingly from the child to the curriculum against which those difficulties are noticeable. As Wedell (1985) puts it:

> The concept of special educational need is a relative one, and need is seen as the outcome of the interaction between the resources and deficiencies of the child, and the resources and deficiencies of his [*sic*] environment.

Such a shift in construction has obviously made many, often threatening, demands on schools and teachers and, not least, on traditionally organized support services.

Supporting change

The changes which LEAs are occupied with in this way are very complex, and they depend as much on the education of attitudes as on structural rearrangement. While this must be true for all changes, it is of particular importance in the realization of the 1981 Act that in its strongest spirit seeks to shift the whole axis of our understanding of special educational needs; the structural changes it entails are minor by comparison. The structures of organization for learning difficulty and 'failure' reflect and reproduce attitudes that are part of a much larger, and even more deeply sedimented, tradition of social order and organization. The task of redefinition of special education is as much a social as an educational one.

Change itself does not happen simply, immediately and unilaterally, but is a much more awkward, less predictable and often painful affair. For the 'old' constructions are embedded deeply in how schools and support services alike typically operate and how they are organized in traditions of practice. Insights are often espoused as functions of policy by LEA members and officers who are relatively ignorant not so much of the facts of school practice as of the attitudes and experiences which lie tacitly at the heart of those practices. In any event, they will not themselves be direct agents of change; this role is likely to fall to advisers and advisory teachers, perhaps to agencies such as the Schools' Psychological Service, and certainly to the support services themselves.

In any LEA reorganizing in this way, the support service is central to these changes, and has a peculiarly complex task. It must both step outside of its own tradition of practice, and persuade others in school to do the same. It must at once educate itself in a new way of working, and schools into different expectations. This is essentially an experimental role, and one concerned with mutual redefinition.

The nature of the task

At the beginning of this chapter, we outlined some of the historical conditions which lie behind the operation of a support service, emphasizing particularly the 'deficit' model of learning (which was usually reading) difficulty which led to a characteristic role for support teachers. Moses *et al.* (1988) provide a sketch of the features typical of these services before the redefinitions of the Warnock Report (GB.DES, 1978) and the 1981 legislation, and the reorganization that followed them. These are:

- the concentration was exclusively, or at least predominantly, upon reading problems;
- the service was principally for primary schools;
- most, if not all, staff of the service taught children with reading problems directly, usually in small groups but sometimes individually;

- children were withdrawn from the classroom for this extra help, which was usually given within the school but sometimes at a separate reading centre. (Moses *et al.*, 1988, p. 74)

In a similar summary of broadly corresponding changes to support services for students with learning difficulties in ordinary schools, they point out that:

the teacher is now a client of the service as well as [is] the pupil; there is a greater orientation towards offering help in the classroom as opposed to withdrawing pupils from it; and a wider range of special [educational] needs than simply reading difficulties are being dealt with. (ibid., p. 84)

The purpose of this section is to consider these shifts in practice as they affect and are affected by the support team itself: What traditions determine its role? How can it develop its options? What are the problems in such developments?

Ten years ago teachers entering a support service for students with learning difficulties knew what to expect, and what was expected of them; they were essentially reading specialists – organizationally located somewhere towards the end of Dessent's line of referred responsibility (see above) – brought in to attend to the special problems of literacy that teachers and their schools could not cope with in the ordinary run of things. Being specialists, they brought with them their battery of instruments: technical devices for assessing, diagnosing and remediating technically identified difficulties. These both justified their presence and created a professional divide between the school and the support teachers. The 'teams' in which they were organized were largely administrative units through which particular support teachers were assigned to particular schools; their tasks were given with the assignment. These tactical responses were characterized by Golby and Gulliver (1979) as an 'ambulance service'; the strategy they thus served was an offensive on individual failure.

Golby and Gulliver's paper was among the first signals of a change in direction for learning support. 'Whose remedies, whose ills?' – as it was called – directed attention explicity to the curriculum as both a source of, and a means of meeting, individual difficulties. There have been various developments of this argument (for example, Swann, 1983; Widlake, 1984; Clough and Thompson, 1987) but the central thesis is a common one: look only slightly beyond the presenting difficulty – the thesis goes – and you will see features of the curriculum closely, and sometimes causally correlated with those problems. As Widlake puts it:

> When 'normal' individuals show an inability to learn in school, yet are perfectly capable of learning in other situations, one should be driven to consider what aspects of the society are creating negative attitudes... any regime which concentrates on their difficulties and ignores their reactions to the turmoil around them is unlikely to be effective, even if feasible. (Widlake, 1984, p.13)

The focus of activity of the last ten years has thus moved towards 'the turmoil'; moved, that is, to the curriculum and to the significance of instances of 'failure' as *responses* to that curriculum.

The Options for Reorganization

The 'new' support service has its orgins in these ideological developments and its new activities can be seen to express a change in the climate of educational thinking. As they were generally constituted before the 1981 Education Act, the support services had a key role in maintaining the model of institutional segregation as they strove to contain low-achieving children within mainstream education. The growing dissatisfaction with this distinction, and the growing evidence of its arbitrary educational and moral basis, threw into question the role of a service inherently involved in ever-presenting individual difficulties unrelated to their broader curricular context. New opportunities for support services follow immediately after blurring of the distinctions between 'ordinary', 'remedial' and 'special' education; the sort of activities that are becoming characteristic of the redefined support services are natural expressions of the redefinitions of learning difficulty and special educational need.

Three interrelated features of the 1981 legislation are particularly relevant. Firstly, the abolition of the statutory categories of handicap, and their replacement with the relative notion of learning difficulties; secondly, the requirement to integrate students with learning difficulties as far as possible within mainstream settings; and thirdly, the recognition of the curriculum as a context for understanding and meeting special educational needs. In each case these elements of policy lead directly to the practical roles which we see emerging in the new support services. Thus the new tasks of the support service are to provide help not so much for individual students as for the institutions and staff involved in realising these changes.

The options available for developing support services in this spirit are not new in themselves; what is novel, however, is the emphasis which is placed on their relative importance. The axes in Figures 1.1 represent the twin continua of the nature and the focus of support service work. Although generic activities could be plotted on any part of this graph, the historical development of the 'new' service is best expressed by the line x, which shows the move away from remediating attention on individuals towards a more consultative role with the whole school – staff and pupils – as its client focus.

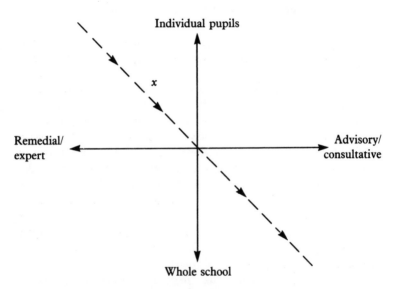

Figure 1.1: The changing role of the support service.

In the case study introduced in Chapter 2, the organization of the team was very clearly and strongly led by the response of the LEA to the ideology of the 1981 Act. Its aims were stated unequivocally in policy documents. The next chapter outlines these developments in more detail.

Chapter 2
City LEA Integration Support Service

In the following chapters we shall make reference to a case study of one LEA's attempt to develop a service for supporting children with special educational needs in the ordinary school. We shall call this authority City LEA and the service which it developed City Integration Support Service (CISS).

City LEA is a large metropolitan authority in the north of England. Like many other authorities it had considered ways of developing its special education system following the publication of the Warnock Report (GB.DES, 1978) and the implementation of the 1981 Education Act (GB.DES, 1981). However, what is of particular interest is that the changes followed a period of debate within the LEA where a philosophy of meeting special educational needs was considered, rather than a situation where the new developments were designed as short-term expedients. In addition the LEA decided that its attempts should be evaluated.

CISS: A Pilot Study

CISS has its origins in the concerns expressed by a variety of people within the LEA following the implementation of the 1981 Education Act. Mainstream schools believed that there were insufficient resources available to implement the Act. This concern can be found, for example, in the minutes of the Schools (Special) Subcommittee for a meeting in July 1984.

A group of first schools stated:

> This governing body views with concern the fact that some pupils
> are having to wait unacceptable lengths of time before being
> assessed by a psychologist and the schools are unable to meet the
> needs of these pupils. It urges the Schools (Special) Subcommittee
> to provide sufficient psychologists to assess these children and
> support schools in accordance with the 1981 Education Act.

There was also concern about resources in a general sense. This
resolution was submitted by the governors of a group of middle
schools:

> ... the governing body of these schools wish to bring to the notice
> of the Schools (Special) Subcommittee the imminent need of
> schools in the area of resources as far as buildings, materials and
> staffing, both teaching and ancillary, to enable the 1981 Education
> Reform Act to be implemented successfully ...

In the years following the 1981 Education Act there were also several
changes in the characteristics of the pupil population, and in the
special schools. The numbers of children on roll fell by 5.2 per cent in
mainstream schools, but by 35.4 per cent in special schools during the
period 1982 to 1988, as Table 2.1 reveals. These figures refer to the
full range of special schools, but it appears that the major change was
in the numbers of children attending schools for children with
moderate learning difficulties. In such schools the reduction in
numbers over the shorter period of 1983 of 1987 ranged from 18 to 54
per cent.

Table 2.1: Full-time pupils on roll in City LEA–special and mainstream

	All special schools	Mainstream schools
1982	1699	83,917
1988	1098	79,591
Fall over six-year period (%)	35.4	5.2

Source: DES Form 7 Figures, submitted by City LEA.

At the same time there was concern about the contribution of
remedial centres, which were perceived to be based upon an

outmoded model of curative intervention over a short period for a small number of children. These centres were considered to offer a narrow curriculum, to remove the ownership of the problem from mainstream schools, and to be too costly.

The numbers of pupils educated out of the authority also fell from 140 in 1981 to 12 in 1987. This had the effect of releasing funds for spending in the LEA's own schools, but presumably the numbers of youngsters with special needs in those schools increased.

During the period of the early to mid-1980s the LEA was developing a number of initiatives. The questions being asked were whether these approaches constituted any kind of coherent plan, and whether they were based upon anything other than a general commitment to integration.

The origin of CISS can be traced to discussion between certain key officers of the authority who had a common philosophical attachment to the belief that children with special educational needs should be educated in mainstream schools. This group comprised the education officer responsible for special education, the adviser for special education and some members of the psychological service. The group held meetings over a period of time to thrash out some ideas derived from the basic philosophical position they shared.

Thus the deliberations of a small group of educationists, committed to a common philosophy, formed the origins of CISS. However, this belief system was recognized as being only the beginning of the process. It is one thing to proclaim a commitment to integration but quite another to put this into operation.

This Study Group, as we shall call them, considered how to implement their ideas within the overall policies of, and resources available within, the LEA. They developed a plan for a support system designed to help children with special educational needs within their local schools. The main focus was not on the reintegration of children removed from the mainstream system, although some might be involved. Rather the plan was to extend support to those children currently in the schools in order to prevent them being removed.

It was recognized that there was a need to evaluate this proposed system, so the authority decided to implement this development within one-quarter of the LEA. The schools were chosen to represent a cross-section of the authority and comprised the following: 3 nursery schools, 34 first schools, 16 middle schools, and 6 upper schools. The total school population was about 21,000.

The Nature of CISS

Aims

The aims of CISS are:

- to ensure coordination of all educational support services, their information and resources;
- to simplify and focus the requests of schools for assistance;
- to allow the more effective use of the Section 11 funded members of all support services, and a more systematic evaluation of the progress of knowledge and skills in meeting the special educational needs of *ethnic minority pupils*;
- to promote a greater chance of maintaining individuals in mainstream through the common aim and corporate consideration of all available information;
- to promote a greater likelihood of change within schools where necessary by the delivery of a consistent, planned approach to problems;
- to facilitate a sequential approach and provide a continuum of intervention and help;
- to enable the exchange of experience between mainstream schools and special schools and other support staff thus extending the expertise of all and increasing career opportunities;
- to promote better assessment and coordination of individual schools' *in-service* requirements;
- to allow the *evaluation* of various modes of intervention.

(NB: All emphases are from the authority's orginal paper)

It can be seen from these aims that the service had a very wide brief. It was intended that the new service should be more efficient and cost-effective than that which it replaced. This would be achieved in a number of ways. Coordination would be improved by having only one service to deal with. The approach to schools would be more consistent and planned, leading to a greater likelihood that necessary changes would be made. There would be a continuum of intervention rather than a dichotomy or restricted choice. The service would not only work with children as primary clients but also with their teachers.

The staffing for this new service was to be derived from the services already in existence, but which would then be replaced. Thus centres were closed, releasing posts to be reallocated to CISS. Other staff were to be seconded from the Remedial Teaching Service, which was to cease operation in the pilot area. Finally staffing was to be diverted from some of the resources of special schools. Overall CISS was to have the equivalent of 17 full-time teachers. Members of the Psychological Service were to have an important working relationship with CISS but were not part of the core team.

Because of the need to finance CISS by diverting existing funds, rather than by having access to new funding, the early entrants to the service were teachers who had been operating in the services mentioned above. Apart from restricting the range of potential applicants generally, this had the particular result that there were no members of the team with an ethnic minority background. Given the large number of children in the LEA who were of Asian origin this was to prove a significant factor.

The evaluation

The evaluation was commissioned to run from the beginning of CISS (January 1987) for a two-year period (until December 1988). In the event a further follow-up survey was conducted in April 1989, and the final report of the evaluation was presented to the LEA's relevant committee in May 1989.

The evaluation took a variety of forms. We took the view that the authority had made a policy decision in terms of the general philosophy that it wished to implement, namely integration of support for children with special educational needs. There was potentially a question concerning this basic ideological position, but our main endeavour was to explore the effects of this policy decision.

Consequently we were much less concerned with comparing CISS with an alternative system than with investigating the nature of CISS itself, and its effect on others. This fitted in with the concerns of the authority. Although they were keen for CISS to succeed they were also open-minded to the possibility that this system might not be the best for delivering the goods.

These considerations led us to a methodology which was largely qualitative. We were interested to discover how CISS was perceived by significant post-holders. However we also recognized that there was a need to provide some information for comparing the operation of CISS with that of other services. Consequently we sought information and conducted standardized surveys of opinion in addition to the structured interviews.

The information we collected is available in a research report (Clough and Lindsay, 1989). It can be summarized as follows:

- Interviews with key personnel at the beginning of CISS.
- Interviews with heads after the first half term.
- Interviews with special educational needs coordinators during the second term.
- A survey of teachers in schools covered by CISS and in non-CISS schools after four terms.
- A survey of heads and special education needs coordinators in CISS schools after nine terms.
- Investigation of the work of support assistants.
- Evaluation of the in-service training offered by CISS.
- Investigation of the team experience.
- Case studies of practice in the operation of CISS in five schools.

Thus we conducted a project that had many points of focus and made use of different types of data, including the observation of practice, structured interviews, questionnaires and document analysis.

The project was also interactive. Although we had a reasonably clear view of the main issues and general directions, we were also keen that the study should be seen as action research. As a result we discussed our findings at several stages during the research with interested parties: the CISS team themselves, the officers and the authority's committee. In addition we reported to an Evaluation Advisory Group which included representatives of the teacher associations as well as to representatives of CISS and the Psychological Service, the responsible education officer, the adviser and an elected member who acted as Chair.

The Use of This Research

The research in City LEA will not be reported at length in this book. We make use of some of the findings from this detailed examination of one LEA's attempts to develop a system of support for children with special educational needs. We use these findings to illuminate a number of issues which arise. We also draw upon the work of others in this field, and upon investigations we have conducted in another city in the north of England.

Chapter 3
Developing the Support Team

The 'new' support services increasingly make demands on their staff that were uncommon in previous forms of organization. Whatever backgrounds staff bring with them to the team, most will be inexperienced in some of the skills expected of them. The new support service, then, must develop these individual strengths while building a cohesive and mutually supportive unit able to meet the infinitely individualized demands of its client schools. In this chapter we outline and discuss some of the possible steps for developing a service of appropriate complexity.

In Chapter 1 we highlighted the emerging features of the supportive principle. The principle is to organize services offering constructive support to work which is in the first and last instances the responsibility of another organization – the school. The support service does not take over the specific problem from the school or teacher, but rather offers help scaled according to the school's needs, the team's repertoire and the pressure on the resources of each. It is indeed an important function of the emerging support ideology that schools see problems as their own (if not necessarily of their own creation, as some critics might argue), and consider the remediation of these problems to be within their own capabilities, albeit with some help. The focus of support activity has thus moved away from individuals and their problems towards the curriculum, and instances of 'failure' are considered to be responses to that curriculum. Such a move cuts the ground from beneath the platform of the traditional support service organization. More particularly, it demands skills and ways of working for which few, if any, support teachers have any training. Anticipating some of these new patterns, Golby and Gulliver (1979) suggested that specialist teachers would need to develop 'a much greater understanding of linguistics and curriculum planning' – but this is probably less than the half of it. Current practice in support services frequently calls for well-developed skills of negotiation, consultation and liaison in often sensitive and difficult situations with a wide range of senior personnel; it demands skill in the design and delivery of staff and curriculum development programmes; it requires familiarity with a broad range of curricular and policy developments; all this in addition to keeping abreast of developments in the fields customarily associated with support for individual learning difficulty. Furthermore, all these changes are taking place within a rapidly changing educational context; one effect of this is that support services themselves may often define the new ground of their activities as they develop. They do not, as in the past, inherit a well-trodden and understood path of practice. They are frequently the cutting edge of emerging policy, required to realize in schools and elsewhere the implications of an ideology drafted at member, officer and advisory levels of the LEA.

Such a demanding agenda clearly calls for levels of skill and particular experience that are seldom found in any one individual; accordingly, team organization in a reflexive programme must address both the demands made of the service from outside, and the development of its own strengths: this is to give a real meaning to 'on-the-job' training!

Strategies for Team Development: The Case of CISS

Like many such services, CISS initially drew most of its workers either from special schools (which were closed or radically re-modelled as part of the Plan for Special Educational Needs) or from the Remedial Teaching Service (which in its traditional organization had played few of the roles called for by the new form of service). In understanding how CISS simultaneously met the development needs of its members and the demands of the client schools, the following factors seem particularly important.

1. The 'ownership of change'

In a sense, the team as such was formed on the job; there was little or no time for the elaborate induction of members and the team came together as it took on its brief. However, its brief was described minimally and was largely structural; the team had to deliver a coordinated support service 'scaled according to need'. It was left very much to the coordinator and team members to develop the scope and character of the work according to the assembled experience and vision of the team members. It has become commonplace to talk of the necessity for professionals' 'ownership' of the issues and processes of change, yet this is undoubtedly what led the CISS to its current form of practice.

2. An experimental design

It is important to remember that CISS was set up provisionally, as a project rather than a tenured organization. The project was initially given two years to develop and demonstrate itself, with no guarantee of an extended life in that form; it had, therefore, an in-built experimental character. This is important in understanding the processes of the CISS team, for this requirement and capacity to be largely self-determining – authors responsible for their own effects – undoubtedly gave both vigour and cohesion to the project. Of course, this might be explained in terms of CISS members' interest in securing their continued employment, but this would be to miss the point of the professionalism and commitment which they brought to their work.

3. The study group

CISS received its initial organizing brief from the LEA via the Study Group (see Chapter 2) which had taken on the task of converting the new principles of supportive education into a framework which would set the stage for what was to follow. Drawing on a range of perspectives, it provided the coordinator with a medium for exploring possibilities. But, most importantly, it did so in a way that still required the team to find its own way within given, broad parameters; it was importantly a *study* rather than a *management* group, and its purpose and usefulness fell away in time with the development of CISS's own identity.

Among other things, the study group identified the need initially to gather information about the organization and the needs of the participating schools (see Chapter 4); it established the idea of forming a contract as the basis for a partnership with schools (see Chapter 6); and it explored the possibilities of In-service Education of Teachers (INSET) for the team, as a means of developing both its cohesion and its collective skills. Of these three areas, the study group contributed most to the design of the information-gathering instrument (the success of which was ambiguous). For the other two areas, the group provided the seeds of ideas and sketches of possible practice, which were left to CISS itself to develop to its own characteristic way of working.

4. Team structure

Although it did not achieve its full complement until some 18 months after starting work, the Plan for Special Educational Needs specified 17 teachers' posts within CISS; in addition to the project coordinator, three assistant coordinators, six senior support teachers and seven support teachers were proposed. The project actually started with its full complement of coordinators and assistants, but with only four senior and two support teachers; one year later, two further senior support teachers were established, and the full complement was achieved a year later. In principle, each post carried different duties and responsibilities, but in practice work was shared equally according to the need for delivery in 37 pre-five and primary, 16 middle and 6 upper schools, and generally reflected the previous school experience of the team members. Initially, the assistant coordinator responsible for each of these three areas of organization was to play a major part in the negotiation of contracts with the CISS schools. The level of subsequent involvement with the school was judged according to the status of the team member; notionally, therefore, a senior support teacher might expect to take more responsibility and initiative than a support teacher.

In practice, however, it soon became clear that this hierarchical organization of the team was more formal than practical; whether work involved liaison with senior management teams on the one hand or direct teaching contact with individual pupils on the other, the distribution of responsibilities tended to follow task-led priorities rather than hierarchical rubrics, and was carried out according to individual strengths.

5. Team INSET

Staff and professional development activities were established very early on in the project, since they were essential to the learning and sharing of skills, and to the creation of a cohesive team. In fact such a high priority was given to INSET that shortly after the establishment of CISS, one-fifth of the week's timetable was set aside for development activities. Additionally, CISS members spent three weekends in the first year on residential courses organized around their identified professional needs.

The INSET programme was varied. Its content was identified partly by the coordinator, but more generally through the stated needs of the team. The most common timetable for the day featured a key input in the morning – not always from an 'outside' speaker – followed by structured opportunities for intra-team consultation in the afternoon.

As well as providing professional development for the team, these sessions had another very important effect: they provided models of INSET organization and processes from which CISS members themselves could critically develop their own skills in identifying, organizing, delivering and evaluating their own school-based INSET programmes. This is not to say that the CISS INSET sessions were always models of good practice; they clearly varied in quality. However – particularly where CISS members substantially participated in or led sessions – they provided something of a laboratory for sharing and exploring forms of INSET which might be adapted for use in schools.

Overall, INSET days were greatly valued as times when the team came together, sharing information and feelings about the progress of the project and the part of individuals in it, hearing and critically exploring what worked in some cases and what did not go quite so well in others; chiefly, sensing and developing the coherence of the team.

6. The contracting system

The system of contracting with schools is dealt with in detail in Chapter 6, but certain of its features are important here to understand how CISS started to develop its now characteristic practice of negotiated intervention with schools.

In terms of structures, the idea of contracting had already been identified by the Study Group as an efficient and productive way of trying to match CISS's strengths with schools' needs; similarly, the requirement for information on the context of these needs led to the introduction of the background information gathering exercise (see Chapter 4).

From the point of view of the newly formed team with its very varied experience of working directly with mainstream school staff, the contracting system clarified their work: it broke down the bewildering size of the CISS brief into manageable units and hence tasks; it allowed them to work initially from the strengths that they already possessed; it made schools responsible for the careful statement of their expectations; and so, in the best application of the term, it provided a measure of mutual accountability which could maximize opportunities for success and highlight areas for further development. Of course in practice the contracting system exposed many problems and discomforts on both sides of the contract, and our discussion in Chapter 6 highlights some of the difficulties as well as the virtues of working in this way. However, as a strategy in establishing a new service the system brought confidence and vigour, which laid a key foundation in the development of CISS's work.

Discussion

Relationships within the team

The team appeared to be highly cohesive. Factors contributing to this cohesion were identified as a willingness to share skills by team members, an openness in the team and an excellent manager. Several team members identified a common thread in CISS that derived from 'a positive agreement on certain things', which it was felt might have been the result of everyone 'building from scratch'. Individual team members appreciated team discussion groups and many saw colleagues as a resource, providing tips and suggestions so that team members were not left to sink or swim. Support was seen as being mutually available at all times and as fostering individual and group development. 'Base' provided a rich source of company and support; relationships were open and relaxed. Some members drew attention to the complete contrast between their experience in 'base' and that in some school staffrooms.

As the year progressed, however, it was increasingly difficult to find time to communicate with colleagues and there was a feeling that not enough time was available for satisfactory input and liaison. Some team members felt, rather against their will, that they were increasingly working in isolation because of the time demands of the work and that there was a need for extra staff or resources. Several team members felt they were frantically trying to keep up with both the pace of change within CISS and the demands of schools, and felt that working in CISS now demanded skills that had not originally been necessary, such as providing INSET. However, team members felt that they had learnt much through working on CISS, had broadened their experience and had increased their knowledge.

Working with schools

In order to work effectively in schools, team members had to cope with demands that stretched their interpersonal skills. They had to acquire the skills to interact with different individuals in the context of organizations which were unfamiliar to them and whose workings were not immediately accessible.

In the initial stages of the project, supportive feelings developed rapidly in the team as members responded to the stress and pressure of being involved in a new enterprise with a 'concerted effort not to fail'. Some experienced difficulties in establishing methods of working with schools 'despite a good induction'. Early contacts with schools were sometimes 'sobering' when staff realized that a path had not necessarily been laid for CISS work. Respondents sometimes experienced problems in becoming established in an unsympathetic or hostile environment, and discovered the implications of entering schools as 'outsiders' and having to 'win staff over' and prove themselves.

Failing to provide the immediate support that schools had expected and the resentment schools expressed about this sometimes led to a feeling that team members were imposing a system on the schools rather than working with them. Other difficulties were experienced in 'learning to work on another's patch', with teachers who were in a senior position, and with schools which felt their ability to solve their own problems was being questioned.

At a later stage CISS staff found themselves negotiating and establishing mutually satisfactory relationships with schools, recognizing the different expectations that heads and teachers in different situations had of them, the necessity for responses to be tailored to situations and the need for clear objectives of involvement to enable CISS and schools to work together. The idea of working together was taken seriously by team members who felt that it was important to communicate that 'they were both – support teacher and class teacher – trying to achieve something' in the interests of the children.

Agreement between the team members and the school was sometimes hindered by their differing opinions about what help CISS should give. This was particularly the case when the CISS member was expected by the school to take over responsibility for the difficulties of children, in which case the team member was seen by the school as being unhelpful when he or she refused to do so. Team members therefore felt they needed adequate time in school to establish relationships 'to build up an idea of what we're about'. Some felt that they should try to fit in with teachers' expectations while others felt that their role was negotiable with the teacher: the end result being that support teachers and class teachers had the same expectations.

CISS team members characterized their work variously in terms of the roles they might play:

- Carriers of good practice.
- Catalysts (aiming to help schools to develop their own approaches and strategies).
- Objective outsiders (providing a view uninfluenced by the pressures of the classroom).
- Curriculum advisers.
- Experts (this term was strongly resisted by some but others felt it reflected reality).
- Identifying with and empowering teachers (helped by previous experience as a teacher).

Generally the team members saw themselves as having developed their interpersonal skills and 'quite high management skills'. Some members identified difficulties related to systems rather than people; for example the problem of finding time in first schools for liaison meetings, the perception of support teachers as servants of the authority, thus representing an unsatisfactory response to the problems identified by schools.

Working within the CISS structure

The approach adopted by the team was a highly structured one. Work in schools was carried out in accordance with the 'aims of CISS' (a set of guidelines) and the contract. The guidelines were seen by some as a useful reference point making clear their objectives in schools. Contracts were also seen as assisting clarity: 'school knows what I'm doing and I know what I'm doing . . . at the review we can both discuss whether it's worked or not'. Contracts formalizing the role of a team member in a school were perceived by some team members as reflecting the school's expressed needs; conversely, they were considered to be too formal and to remove 'room for manoeuvre' by others. The formality of numbered forms and the proliferation of paperwork also concerned some: 'We're not into being business people, we're into being helpful people'.

The negotiation of a contract with schools was usually carried out by assistant coordinators and sometimes by senior support teachers, but concern was expressed by support teachers who felt that those who were going to do the work should be involved in the planning and negotiation stages.

Despite the fact that CISS's structure was strongly hierarchical, members commented that this did not intrude in their work: 'Half the time we're not really aware of it'. However, some felt that smaller teams might help to reduce the communication problem and facilitate the democratic sharing of responsibilities.

There were concerns that the structure of CISS produced a duplication of resources and that the kind of recruit needed by CISS would not be attracted by the main professional grade posts on offer. There was therefore an argument for merging the roles of senior support teachers and support teachers. This, it was hoped, would reduce the workload of senior support teachers, reduce contract negotiation time and give support teachers access to areas of greater responsibility. Some members, however, felt that it was sometimes better not to make 'on the spot' decisions and that a delay could be legitimized if consultation with a higher status member of staff was necessary.

The ethos of CISS was seen as embodying a commitment to monitoring and review; some saw this as necessitating a structured approach that clarified the nature of problems and the strategies to remediate them. The personal development resulting from this type of approach was valued by a number of team members who felt that their own thinking had become clearer and more precise as a result.

Members of the team also felt that they had gained a breadth of experience in working across the age range in different situations. The variety of individual experiences within the team was also seen as valuable, enabling a flexible and appropriate response. A number of team members felt that a skilled management had the effect of increasing their own ability to enable others. For many, good and effective team management was seen as being fundamental to team success.

In studying the team experience, we found much to applaud in its organization and ethos. The team – both collectively and individually – appeared to have met a large agenda of demands, a new set of roles and a weight of expectations with efficiency, imagination and industry. The pressures placed on the team – some of which are endemic to support work – produced stresses which were in the main channelled towards creative and palpable ends.

In addition to comments made by team members, three features of team organization seemed particularly salient to us. Firstly, the team benefited from the energies of a remarkable coordinator, who was able to give positive, supportive leadership as well as being sensitive to the development of individual strengths and interpretations of role. Secondly, the cohesion of the team was established and developed through a regular programme of INSET activities aimed at developing specific skills and techniques within the team, but also providing a forum for supportive and critical self-appraisal by the team. The planned provision of this sort of activity seems to us to have been an essential determinant of the team's success. Thirdly, it is difficult to avoid speculating about the effect of the gender imbalance within the team – which was predominantly female; we were certainly aware of a quality of mutual support which would perhaps be unusual in any male dominated team, whatever the context.

Comment

The CISS team had its own particular context and composition and to understand its workings, its successes and its shortcomings fully it would be necessary to look at the much wider set of political contexts – both within and without the team itself – which gave the project its purposes and influenced its effects. However, in this chapter we have attempted to highlight some of the structures of team organization and development which would be recognizable and significant in the life of any support service.

Chapter 4
Gathering Information

In this chapter we will examine the capability of special needs support systems for information gathering, for unless this is adequate and the information gained is accurate the whole system will lack a sound foundation. In computer jargon it will be an example of GIGO – garbage in, garbage out.

We will examine this issue at different levels. At one level there is the detailed information required to determine a child's particular status, in terms of his or her strengths, weaknesses, interests, hopes and fears. At the other end of the continuum is the LEA's need for information on the prevalence of problems, the functioning of its provision and the opinions of consumers and others, such as elected members. Between these is the level of the school.

At each level in this system different decisions have to be made, and hence a variety of information will be required. In the following section we consider these issues in more detail.

Information About the Child

The view expressed in the Warnock Report (GB.DES, 1978), that up to about one in five children might have special educational needs at some stage in their schooling, is now generally accepted. It is worth remembering that this is not an immutable 'fact' but rather an hypothesis derived from research studies. These studies made use of different methods to determine children's difficulties in development but ultimately judgements were made in terms of cut-off points: OK – not OK. For example, one of the studies which guided the Warnock Committee was the Isle of Wight study (Rutter *et al.*, 1970). One criterion they used was a reading age that was at least 28 months below chronological age on the *Neale Analysis of Reading Ability* (Neale, 1957). This cut-off was chosen relative to the age of the children being investigated – 9- to 10-year-olds; therefore the '28 months' was a relative concept. Unfortunately, as time passes, the relative nature of these criteria is forgotten. An interesting account of this process, using tests to determine special school placement, is provided by Gipps *et al.* (1985).

However, although we would express a warning about the '20 per cent' of children deemed to have special educational needs, we would concede that it is useful to consider the incidence as being of this order, rather than the 'two per cent' which used to be the rough estimate. The suggestion that we should consider a much wider group than those with severe–profound impairments is, we believe, one to support.

But this conceptualization has implications for the process of identifying children's problems and hence their needs. Although this is essentially a difference in scale rather than type we suggest that there are greater problems.

For the present purposes we shall consider the 'two per cent' and the '18 per cent' separately. We stress this is for illustration only at this point and support the Warnock view that there is a continuum of need. We shall return to the issue of the boundary between the two 'groups' subsequently.

The 'two per cent'

The population
A high proportion of children with severe and profound sensory impairments and physical disabilities will be identified well before school age. Lindsay (1984) has reviewed the methods used to detect these problems. For example, severe hearing loss should be detected within the child's first year of life. Similarly children with severe and profound intellectual impairment will usually be identified in the pre-school period.

Recently there have been many examples of good practice in both identifying and providing for these youngsters. The *Portage* Scheme, for example, has been extended across many LEAs and has become a welcome support to children and to their parents (see Hedderley and Jennings, 1987).

However, the majority of children who traditionally have been considered as part of this 'two per cent' are those with moderate difficulties and, to a lesser extent, those with behavioural difficulties. The large majority of these children are not assessed as having special needs until they are in the school system. Thus, even within the so-called 'two per cent' we find an important distinction between children in terms of identification.

However, as LEAs develop provision to meet the needs of some of these children, more will be identified at the pre-school stage and be given access to nursery provision. The development of such provision in one LEA has been described and evaluated by Lindsay and Desforges (1986).

Information

Children with severe and profound impairment invariably require a detailed assessment that involves a number of professionals along with the parents. Many will have medical conditions which are either primary or secondary to their learning difficulties. For example, children with Down's Syndrome frequently have heart defects. Those with hearing losses will need detailed assessments by audiologists. Psychologists will contribute information on the child's development. Whereas this was at one time limited to an IQ test and a few general statements, nowadays it should include a more extensive analysis, of cognitive abilities (see Lindsay, 1989).

Pre-school support teachers, social workers, health visitors, general practitioners and speech therapists are all frequently involved in these assessments. Lastly there is the important information provided by parents on the child's developmental history and current functioning in the home and other environments.

Recent practice in pre-school teams and networks of services, given extra impetus by the 1981 Education Act (GB.DES, 1981), has developed to a high standard in many parts of the country. The issue for schools, therefore, is not one of identification *per se* but of ensuring that the information available is communicated to them and used appropriately. Unfortunately links between these pre-school services and schools are not always good.

For children identified at school age there is an important extra stage for the school to undertake – the identification of the *need* to assess. This is not a simple decision. Formal assessments under the

1981 Education Act, for example, are long, time-consuming affairs taking up significant resources. Inappropriate assessments are to be avoided. But, and here is the paradox, how can we decide who should be assessed before the assessment has been carried out?

Traditionally this problem has been met by the use of screening procedures. For example, children might receive medical screening, including tests of vision and hearing, early in their school lives. They will be rather general methods of assessment but, hopefully, fine enough to distinguish those who have a high likelihood of a problem. Lindsay (1984) has reviewed such screening methods. While some are indeed accurate and useful, there are limitations. However, in our concern for the 'two per cent' this is less of an issue than, as we shall see below, when the '18 per cent' is considered. Indeed, evidence is accumulating to suggest that, given access to the children, many problems can be identified and assessed reasonably accurately (see Stevenson, 1984).

However, it is important for schools to have a system of reviewing all the children from the age of five (or below, in nursery schools and units) and identify which children present such significant difficulties that a *detailed* assessment is required. The use of an instrument at age five, such as the *Infant Rating Scale* (Lindsay, 1981), is one way to carry out this process.

The *Infant Rating Scale* (*IRS*) for five-year-olds comprises 25 items divided into five subscales: language, early learning, behaviour, social integration and general development (see Table 4.1). The teacher can screen the class and identify children who achieve particularly low scores (within the bottom two per cent approximately) either on specific items, subscales or the total score.

There is also a version for seven-year-olds, and a new instrument for children of 8 to 11 years, the *Junior Rating Scale* (Abraham and Lindsay, 1990). These instruments aid the teacher in identifying which children might require further, detailed assessment and give preliminary pointers towards the types of difficulties the children are having.

The '18 per cent'

Although there is now general acceptance of the view that the group of children with special educational needs is larger than the traditional

Table 4.1: *Infant Rating Scale* **level 1: composition of subscales**

Subscale	Items
1. *Language*	Expressive language: articulation, vocabulary, sentence construction, expression Receptive language: comprehension of instructions, understanding of words, memory for oral information
2. *Early learning*	Basic skills: fine coordination and manipulation, drawing, writing, matching and early reading, number Attitude to learning: concentration and ability to organize, approach to learning, attention and distractibility
3. *Behaviour*	Temperament, attitude to teacher, kindness to peers
4. *Social integration*	Participation in class activity, acceptance by peers, desire to mix
5. *General development*	Gross motor skills, maturity, response to new situations, level of concern felt

'two per cent', there are difficulties in determining both exactly who these children are, and what their problems might be.

This group of children includes that large group whose progress is sufficiently slow, or in some cases deviant, to cause concern to teachers and parents. The traditional yardstick in schools has been reading development and, to a lesser extent, general intelligence as assessed by standardized tests. The group also includes children who exhibit behavioural problems and those with milder degrees of sensory and physical impairment (for example the 'clumsy child').

The nature of difficulties exhibited by children is now usually acknowledged to be the result of an interaction between their own strengths and weaknesses, and the degree of support offered by the environment. This process has been termed 'compensatory interaction' (see Wedell and Lindsay, 1980) and is presented diagrammatically in Figure 4.1. Note also that there is a time dimension – the relative relationships between the different factors might vary over time.

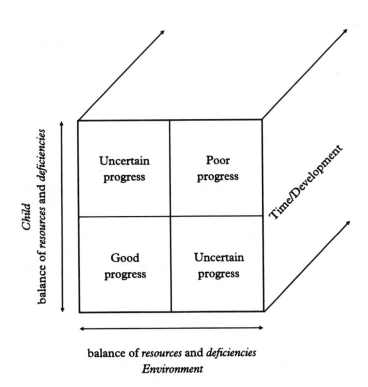

Figure 4.1: Compensatory interaction. *Source:* Wedell and Lindsay (1980).

It is also evident that the definition of these children is even more relativistic – slower than whom? More difficult behaviour than what level? Consequently, different schools have different definitions of which children should be in this group.

For children with severe and profound impairments, there is clearly a very significant 'within-child' element to the causation of the problem. This is not to suggest that this is the only factor to consider, since the family and school support systems will still make a great deal of difference to the development of these children. However, with the '18 per cent' the evidence for within-child variables as the major causative factors is less strong. On the contrary, it has been shown that there is a large overlap between children in this group and those in the normal population on a range of measures (such as IQ and basic attainments).

This poses serious problems for any system of identification. Results of studies (for example Lindsay, 1979) that have followed children through their infant schools have demonstrated the relative unpredictability of many children, particularly those in the group under consideration here. Whereas some who are 'at risk' at five years continue to have problems at, say, seven, others do not. While there is a problem of disentangling the relative effects of any defects in the measuring instruments from true child variation, there is support for the latter being a major factor.

The Bullock Committee (GB.DES, 1975) suggested that screening at five years would be useful in determining which children required help before they started to fail within the school system. However, it is now clear that this is not a simple task. On the contrary, several studies have now demonstrated the differential progress of children which is related to school effects in addition to any intrinsic abilities the child might show before entering school (see Mortimore *et al.*, 1988; Tizard *et al.*, 1988; see also Lindsay, 1988, for a review).

For example, Mortimore *et al.* (1988) investigated the progress of nearly 2000 children over four years in 50 schools in London. Although the attainments of the children were related to factors such as social class, there was also evidence that the children's progress was related to which school they attended. Mortimore *et al.* have also investigated school factors, and suggest those which appear to be related to more satisfactory progress. The study of Tizard *et al.* (1988) was similar but investigated younger children from the end of nursery school into infant school.

The consequences of such research are that for this group of children it is essential to investigate the *school* factors. Whilst these should be considered for all children with special needs in terms of *intervention* for the '18 per cent', it may be that school factors take on a greater importance in terms of the *causality* of the child's problems.

Information About the Total System

The LEA must be in a position to monitor the system of special educational support it has set up. This is often not carried out comprehensively. Statistics on the numbers of children receiving different forms of support, and the relative costs of these provisions, are not always monitored carefully.

For example, the review of special education provision in a large LEA which involved one of us (GL) during the early part of 1990 revealed a major lack of readily available data. Although the authority had a computerized data base system, the hard-pressed staff in its pupils' division had not yet found time to load existing data, and indeed were barely keeping up with the inputting of information produced each week. Consequently, the review team's analysis of trends of referrals, for example, was reliant upon a visual search of manual records, a very time-consuming task. Furthermore, the data base, while useful for some tasks, would not allow easy access to the kinds of statistics necessary for LEA-wide perspectives.

A recent review by Swann (1989) has revealed wide variations in the use of different facilities by LEAs. For example, the take-up of places in schools outside the LEA, which has high attendant costs, varied greatly in 1987 from 0.6 per 10,000 to 41.6 per 10,000. Although some difference is to be expected there must be a question mark over this degree of variation. Could LEAs make better use of their funds by ensuring that such provision is made within their boundaries? If we look at the use of non-maintained (private) special schools we find a similar variation. In 1987 take-up of these places varied from a high of 56.4 per 10,000 (Redbridge) to a low of 2.8 per 10,000 (Sheffield).

The costs of transport can also be very high. It is also the case that provision costs can simply grow until a budget is exhausted. At this point the next child to appear will not receive the provision. This happened in the case of support assistants in the schools of City LEA (see Chapter 8) and is happening to many LEAs across the country.

LEAs are not alone in their limited collection and use of information as a guide to planning. A recent report of the Education Science and Arts Committee of the House of Commons (House of Commons, 1987) was also critical of the Department of Education and Science:

The ability of the DES to monitor the implementation of the Act for the purpose of giving guidance is, however, restricted by the paucity of the information it collects. (para. 47)

But there is no point in collecting information unless it has a purpose. For there to be a purpose, in our view, the LEA should have a clear policy. The information which is needed, therefore, will be that which informs the authority how its policy is working. The concern, however, is that LEAs often do not have such policies, let alone adequate monitoring systems. For example, a recent report by Her Majesty's Inspectors (HMI) on the education of physically disabled children was critical of this (GB.DES, 1989). What HMI discovered in their visits to 35 schools and 12 integrated resources was a development almost by default. As more children were integrated into mainstream schools, there were significant negative effects on the viability and nature of the experiences provided within these particular special schools. It appeared that the effects of these developments had not been fully appreciated by the authorities.

The report by HMI on Support Services for Special Educational Needs (GB.DES, 1989) makes similar points, and the report of the House of Commons Committee mentioned above also castigates LEAs for their lack of overall policies.

The City Study

City LEA had a set of well articulated intentions when it set up CISS and the aims of the service were clearly set out (see page 12). There were still some concerns from the field, particularly about the extent to which integration should occur (for *all* children?) and whether the money to pay for it would be available. However, the planning of CISS put much emphasis on policy formulation, setting clear aims and objectives, and monitoring.

One example of this was the basic information gathering exercise, set up to obtain detailed information about the school, since it is the context, as described above. In this case, however, it was not the school analysing itself, but an outside support agency asking for information to enable it to function adequately. This is, of course, a subtle difference and the exercise was not, in the event, unproblematic.

The questionnaire

The method chosen by the CISS team was a detailed questionnaire. This was sent to heads in the early days of the new service, which started in the January. The aims of this information gathering exercise were as follows:

- Formulating a picture of the school's needs and the facilities/resources required.
- Providing the basis for the negotiated contract with schools.
- CISS staff 'getting to know' the schools in the project.
- Helping schools to gather information systematically to meet their own accountability.
- Systematizing support service involvement in schools.
- Informing the support services of overall developments in special educational needs.

The questionnaire comprised five sections:

1. Teachers, pupils, teaching groups
This section was concerned with basic demographic features of the school population (such as numbers of pupils and teachers) and the rationale employed for dividing the school population into teaching groups/classes.

2. The role of the special educational needs coordinator
This section was two pages long and required information about the coordinator; for example the salary scale of the special needs coordinator and whether the role had protected time attached to it.

3. School policy documents
This short section of one page asked whether the school had policy documents in seven named areas (such as language and reading, special educational needs) and requested a copy for reference purposes.

4. Untitled
This section (37 pages) had no title, but was a collection of questions relating to record keeping and requested information about methods used in teaching.

- Area of interest:
  Bilingual pupils with special educational needs (one page)
  Behavioural/management (four pages)

- Teaching approaches:
  Cross curricular (one page)
  Maths (four pages)
  Reading (five pages)
  Handwriting (five pages)
  Spelling (five pages)
  Language policy and practice (one page)
  Special educational needs (two pages)

- Records
  General records (three pages)
  Class based records (three pages)
  SEN coordinators (two pages)
  Identification of SEN (one page)

Sections 1–4 of the questionnaire were to be completed by a CISS team member during a period of 2–3 days which was allocated for the specific purpose of familiarization.

A further section was given to the head with a request that on completion it should be returned to CISS. This was known as the 'Headteacher's Questionnaire'. (A modified version went to secondary schools.)

The head's questionnaire
This was a 16-page document with the following sections:

- Area:
  Access across the curriculum.
  Support teachers in school.

- External support to schools:
  Educational support service.
  Non-educational support service.
  External support required but not available at present.
  Pupils returning from special schools.
  Liaison with special schools.
  Pupils with statements and assessments under Section 5.

Use of ancillary staff with pupils who have special educational needs.

Adults in school (ancillary).

Use of other adults/young volunteers in school.

School buildings.

Segregation.

What areas could CISS help with? (checklist to be ticked).

What priority level does special educational needs have in the development plan for the school (six boxes provided for heads to write in their responses).

Special educational needs and other contemporary issues – a list of current issues.

The Response

a) Heads

We interviewed a total of 20 first and middle school heads (approximately a two-thirds random sample) about a month after CISS began. Further interviews were conducted with these schools' special educational needs coordinators in the period from April to September of that year, that is after one to two terms. It was not possible to interview in five first schools, which left a sample of 24 coordinators (who were the teachers with most contact with CISS to date).

The majority of heads made criticisms about the information gathering that CISS staff carried out prior to negotiating contracts with schools: 85 per cent of first school heads and 67 per cent of middle school heads. Also, those first school heads who did make criticisms tended to do so significantly more than their middle school colleagues.

The main criticisms were as follows.

1. Applicability

First schools particularly considered that significant parts of the questionnaire were not applicable to them: 'The first question shows a lack of understanding of first schools where all the teachers are responsible for access to the curriculum'.

2. Difficulty in understanding or completing

About a third of the first school heads made specific reference to this. Apart from references to ambiguities in the questions, the main criticism from first and middle schools was the difficulty in quantifying such aspects as pastoral help and hours per month of external support.

3. Time

Many heads criticized the process as time-consuming. Some were prepared to reserve judgement to see whether the time expended was matched by resources allocated later.

4. Pressure on heads

Some heads, particularly in first schools, did not see why the questionnaires need to be so wide ranging, asking questions about issues these heads did not see as relevant to special needs in any direct way. Some saw the amount of information required as another pressure on heads: 'formidable and threatening'; 'a complicated test you have to pass to qualify for help'.

5. The use of the information

Two heads wondered whether the information given could work against their schools when it came to allocating CISS resources, and identified a temptation to be 'less than frank' – for example would a school with a number of parents involved in the school, because of their good practice, be less likely to receive support from CISS?

6. The questionnaire format

A significant minority were critical of the questionnaire. Five first school heads would all have preferred a less structured format and felt that what they considered to be a highly structured impersonal method did not result in a 'true' picture of what a school was really like. Some had tried to achieve this by completing the questionnaire with the CISS teacher.

Some heads were critical of its style: 'admin-centred rather than geared to helping us'; 'verbose, interminable bumf'.

This study was undertaken at a difficult time for the teaching profession, with its long-running pay dispute. The negative response to the information gathering exercise reflects this in part. Heads were concerned about any extra service requiring more work of them and/ or their staff, rather than offering assistance to the children. Many saw the questionnaire as time-consuming and had other criticisms. They were concerned also that they were having to *give* to CISS (information, their time) when they had expected to *receive* a service from CISS.

b) Special needs coordinators (SENCs)

The SENCs were interviewed one to two terms after the start of CISS. From their reactions, therefore, we gained a view of the information gathering exercise that had the benefit of hindsight from coordinators who had experienced what CISS had actually done.

We asked the SENCs to suggest both the benefits and criticisms of the exercise. The following replies were received (with the number of SENCs making this observation in parentheses).

Benefits
1. It helped the school to prioritize its concerns. (7)
2. It allowed the CISS team members and the schoolteachers to get to know each other. (5)
3. It raised teacher awareness. (4)

Three of the SENCs added that they thought CISS needed to have information.

Criticisms
1. It was too time-consuming. (14)
2. A questionnaire is not a good way to get an accurate picture of the school. (4)
3. Discussion would have given a better picture of the school. (4) (This does not include any of those who made the previous criticism.)
4. More time in classrooms would have given a better picture of the school. (2)
5. Both 3 and 4. (1)
6. Teachers felt they were under critical scrutiny. (3)
7. The school already knew what it wanted from CISS. (2)
8. Too much time elapsed before any help was offered. (2)

In three schools the teachers interviewed said they had not been involved in the information gathering and were unable to comment on it.

The SENCs made other criticisms of the setting up of CISS, including the amount of information available initially and the loss of previous support while CISS got off the ground. However, criticisms about loss of support and information pre-CISS were neither as numerous nor as strongly expressed as criticisms about the information gathering done by CISS. Ten of the SENCs said that the information gathering had not been in any way beneficial for the school. The most commonly and strongly expressed criticism was the time taken, especially in completing the questionnaires. Certainly an allied criticism was that of the unsuitability of a questionnaire to give a true reflection of a school.

It is clear that collecting the information in this way did cause significant concern to the 20 SENCs who were involved. Of these, only four appeared, on balance, to be reasonably satisfied with it. One of these did complain that it was time-consuming, but felt that CISS did need to have the information.

Thus both heads and SENCs were critical of the information gathering exercise. Although the benefits to CISS of collecting information were acknowledged, these respondents saw the balance tipped against such an exercise, at least in this form. Rather, the heads and SENCs tended to prefer an open-ended discussion.

However, another important issue is revealed by this study. The heads and SENCs were expecting to receive a new service. As they saw it, this did not happen initially. On the contrary, they lost the previous support and 'gained' a burden – they had to supply information. To do this required time from themselves and their staffs and, in the short term, there was no pay-off. To make matters worse, the questions asked were seen by some as outside their view of legitimate inquiries. What were seen by the CISS team as useful questions to derive contextual information about the school's policies and resources were seen by some as impertinent intrusions.

Conclusions

We have argued in this chapter for the need for full information if special needs are to be met. As we proclaim the importance of conceptualizing the child's special needs in a context, we have suggested that information must be available about the child, the school and the LEA system(s) as a whole. Not all this information will be required in every case. However, to meet an individual's needs it is necessary to have some information about each level. Not only must we know the child's strengths and weaknesses but also those of the school, and then we can *match* the child's needs with what the school can provide. If the match is imperfect, the child's needs must be considered against the resources available more widely. These might include other schools. But equally they might be support within his or her present school. However, the latter is also part of the LEA's total provision.

The gathering of information must be guided by a purpose. Both the nature of the data and the method of collection will vary with the level concerned. We have focused in this chapter on the collection of data by support services from schools. Several implications can be drawn.

First, the collection of information must be seen as useful and necessary by the giver. If the head, for example, sees it as an unwelcome exercise it will cause resentment. Worse, as we found in our research in City LEA, this resentment can negatively affect opinions of the service as a whole.

We suggest, therefore, that information gathering should have the following characteristics.

1. Negotiation
The first, main recommendation is that information gathering be negotiated. In City LEA it was devised by the people wanting the data, and the suppliers had no say in this. We suggest that it be seen as a collaborative exercise. To this end, information gathering should be part of an interactive process.

2. Interview
To aid this, we suggest that the main method used should be face-to-face interaction, the interview. Here the opportunity for true negotiation can occur. Also, the greater flexibility such a method allows results in a greater likelihood of relevant information being collected. To aid the interview, a structured checklist can be helpful, but should not predetermine the process.

3. Rationale of information gathering
It is important that the schools see the process as necessary. This is aided by the process we recommend, since this can be explained. Moreover, it is still important for the collector of information to focus attention only upon that which is important, and be able to justify this. Also sensitivity is required in explaining why such data might be useful and not simply intrusive.

4. *From information gathering to action*

Finally, it is important that the school does not see the exercise as getting in the way of action. Teachers recognize the need for support agencies to have information, but they want action. Consequently this process of data gathering should be as speedy as possible and the provision of a service should be disrupted as little as possible.

This is less easy, of course, with a new service, particularly if it replaces another service. However, again, the interview as a method allows this issue to be raised and reconciled.

Although we have focused here on one part of the total range of information gathering procedures, there are clear implications for other parts of the system. For example, LEAs should avoid sending questionnaires to schools to collect data and use face-to-face inter- views whenever possible. When this is not necessary, or possible, a clear rationale of the purpose should be made. Similarly, we favour professionals collecting information from colleagues in this way rather than sending forms to be completed. In our experience such forms are often unsuitable for most children in the sense that they either miss the point (under-inclusion) or contain questions about every possible factor which might be relevant (over-inclusion). Again, whenever possible, we recommend the face-to-face interview.

Thus, information is important for several purposes. The teacher needs specific information to teach the child. Support services need a broader range of information to plan and deliver their help. This will include information about the child and the school. The LEA requires its own data to judge trends. The evidence available nationally suggests that data collection is not well developed as a process. Our study of City LEA revealed how a more coherent data collection system could still face difficulties in its implementation. In our view it is necessary to be both clear and concise in the data demands being made, and 'user-friendly' in the collection of the necessary information.

Chapter 5
The Coordination of Services

The successful provision of resources for meeting the special educational needs of children requires planning followed by monitoring of service delivery. The developments of the past five to ten years have made these issues even more important.

In the past special education was, at one level, a relatively simple affair. The majority of children with special educational needs received help within their own school, if at all, from *the* remedial teacher. In primary schools this was often a part-time teacher who took small groups. In secondary schools there might be a 'remedial department', often with only one teacher, and even here not always with full-time responsibility for this role.

A small number of pupils were transferred out of the mainstream school into special schools. Here they came under a different regime, but were still comparable to mainstream pupils in that they were on the roll of a school.

The debate concerning how 'good' or 'right' these arrangements were is considered elsewhere (see Golby and Gulliver, 1979). For the present our concern is to consider the issue of provision from the standpoint of organization and efficiency. As we shall see, more recent developments have greatly increased the complexity of the system. Consequently the issues of planning coordination and monitoring have become more important.

The Development of a Variety of Provision

Although a simple description of the past situation has been provided in the introduction to this chapter, there has been a more complex scenario in recent years. The following factors have contributed to this.

Remedial services

Many LEAs developed peripatetic services to supplement or serve the same function as school-based remedial teachers. These varied considerably in their number of personnel. (For example, in the early 1970s one northern city had one person called 'The Remedial Teacher'!)

The rationale for this development was twofold. Firstly, it was considered more efficient to concentrate expertise within a few people. This could be justified, possibly, if these teachers were indeed experienced and trained. This was the case with some LEAs who had staff development programmes. However, in other cases the staff were recruited from mainstream schools with no training.

Secondly, this could be cost-effective if there were few children requiring such assistance in any one school. The teacher could travel to several schools in a week helping a large number of children in real need.

Units

The second main development was that of units attached to mainstream schools. Provision for hearing impaired children was one of the main leaders in this field with a history of such units stretching back over many years.

Although part of the rationale was educational, in the sense of access to mainstream pupils and curriculum, there was also a major financial factor. Particularly for the less prevalent impairments (hearing for example) it was very expensive to provide special schools. These would often need to be residential, given the distances between children, particularly in country areas.

The provision of units, particularly for hearing impaired children, would often be part of a larger service which also supported individual children in their local schools. Thus one large LEA, for example, caters for between 300 and 400 hearing impaired youngsters. The provision varies from units attached to mainstream schools, to children attending their local schools with limited support from a peripatetic teacher of the hearing impaired. There is, however, an even finer variation in provision than this description suggests. Some units are attached to special schools and cater for children with multiple disabilities; others are attached to mainstream schools, but the pupils' amount of integration forms a minority of their time; while a third group of units serves more as a resource base within their schools, with children integrated into mainstream classes up to almost 100 per cent of their time. Similarly, children in mainstream schools may have a full-time support assistant, as in one case we observed, through the more usual hour or so per week from a teacher of the hearing impaired, to occasional monitoring.

The Benefits and Drawbacks

The development of these two additional forms of provision was rarely part of the overall plan of an LEA and certainly did not feature at national level. The origins of a new service or unit might be found in a number of sources. Below are two possible, though imaginary, scenarios:

1. The drive to integration

Countyshire had a relatively small amount of provision for children with SEN. This had largely been of the form of day special schools for a small number of pupils, particularly those now described as having moderate hearing difficulties. Children with sensory impairments and physical disabilities which are severe or profound were sent out of the county to specialist residential schools. Children with emotional or behavioural difficulties were either 'supported in mainstream' or in extreme cases sent to residential schools for maladjusted children, mainly on the south coast.

The authority received an increase in complaints and agitation from parents who believed that their children's needs were not being met. Some did not want their children to go to boarding schools, while others had been offered no extra provision. The local press had run a series of stories on the plight of these children.

At this time, new staff in the department included an assistant education officer (AEO) for special education. This AEO had been impressed by the arguments for integration. The arrival was warmly welcomed by the principal psychologist who was also keen to develop integrated provision.

Over the next few years these two officers formed a focus for the development of more provision that was in-county, and within mainstream schools. Local councillors also became interested, 7nfluenced in part by one of their number who had a young disabled child and who was shocked by the lack of provision available.

2. The over-provision of segregated schools

Goodborough was an urban authority with a long history of providing for children with SEN. As the traditional approach had favoured concentrating resources in special schools, Goodborough had a large number of such segregated establishments. Indeed it had schools for all the major categories of handicap which the DES had specified.

However, recent trends had posed problems for Goodborough. There had been a significant drop in the birth rate. Furthermore, the developments in perinatal care had reduced the prevalence of some types of disability (although there had also been an increase in some categories of more profoundly impaired youngsters). The officers and councillors were also aware of the changing philosophy concerning the segregation of children. Their former approach, which rendered the authority a provider of special education for other LEAs, was now being questioned. Also, moves towards integration by LEAs such as Countyshire had reduced the numbers of pupils available for its schools.

Within the LEA also, parents, schools and educational psychologists were all expressing a preference for integrated provision. As a result, the referral of children to special schools was reducing.

As a result of following these trends, the absolute numbers of children in the special schools had reduced. Consequently, unit costs had risen dramatically and in some schools teachers had very small classes. Some discontent was being expressed by teachers in disadvantaged mainstream schools in particular, that their task was more difficult than that of their colleagues.

As a result, the LEA set about rationalizing its special school system. It was reluctant to lose the buildings but was able to make modifications to allow schools to change their roles. One boarding school was changed to cater for children with emotional and behavioural difficulties. A spin-off was that the number of children supported out-of-city was reduced dramatically, off-setting costs.

The opportunity was also taken to develop a *support teacher* system, as advocated in the Warnock Report (GB.DES, 1978). The candidates were teachers who had been working within special schools who would now be peripatetic. This was seen as within the spirit of supporting children in mainstream schools – it also made a useful and necessary reduction in the staff of schools which had to be reduced in size.

Similarly, as some schools were closed, integrated units or resources were opened in mainstream schools across the LEA. These also provided job opportunities for the staff of the closed special schools, and provided integrated support for children with special needs.

These two scenarios are not 'real'. They are, however, drawn heavily from reality in several LEAs. They reveal the mixed origins of educational change – philosophical, pragmatic, expedient, bowing to pressure.

These kinds of changes were happening across the country in the late 1970s and early 1980s. The publication of the Warnock Report accentuated and gave more force to a change already evident.

In Chapter 12 we consider some of the educational questions about these developments. But what of the organizational implications?

As LEAs developed these ranges of service they added at least one layer of complexity. In addition, the size of the services in question, including those previously existing, have also increased. Thirdly, new officers have been appointed to deal with these and associated developments [for example the 1981 Education Act (GB.DES, 1981)].

Whereas 10 or 20 years ago there would be a small number of professionals dealing with the children, there are now a large number of different professionals, and the children are receiving a wider range of services. To add to the complexity, if not confusion, the names of the services often vary. For example, Gipps *et al.* (1987) report 35 alternative titles among LEAs for the support services.

The Cascade Model for provision is now well known and often quoted. This is shown in Figure 5.1. It was first used to demonstrate the range of services that can be delineated depending upon the type

---

1. Ordinary class, no special help
2. Ordinary class and ancillary help on care side
3. Ordinary class as base and resource room part-time
4. Special class (base) part-time
   Ordinary class part-time
5. Special class full-time
6. Day special school formally linked (e.g. same campus) to mainstream school
7. Day special school, no such link
8. Residential special school

Figure 5.1: Range of special education provision

of needs a child might have. More recently, Fish (1989) has provided a fuller consideration of provision which will be discussed in Chapter 12. However, rather than use this model to describe the range, we wish to emphasize here the *effect* this range of provision has within one LEA (there is a further dimension if we consider cross-LEA collaboration in planning).

This range of provision requires an impressive number of different services. If the LEA is to act in an efficient manner there must be some means of coordinating these services. By coordination we refer to several aspects: the assessment of the child's needs; the delivery of a particular service; the delivery of several services; the monitoring and review of the provision.

Review

The study by Gipps *et al.* (1987) made a number of comments about the coordination of provision for children with SEN. However, their focus concentrated mainly upon the *liaison* between the class teacher of a child in a mainstream school and visiting special needs teachers. Their study reveals that a continuing worry for teachers is the question of how to find time to liaise. At one extreme Gipps *et al.* report that for one LEA 'teacher dissatisfaction [with the support service] was partly because of poor liaison' (p. 71). However, they also found good practice and, when considering the withdrawal of children by visiting teachers, they suggest that good liaison was occurring.

Gipps *et al*. (1987) have much less to report upon the general issue of liaison, but the authors do conclude:

> Where children were getting a good deal it was where services had been developed in a spirit of co-operation between teachers and the LEA. (p. 135)

In the more detailed accounts of their case studies Gross and Gipps (1987) give more substance to this assertion. They report some LEAs where insufficient thought was given to liaison between support teachers and mainstream teachers, and also where different services had failed to coordinate their activities. Muncey (1989) reinforces this point when he argues for the need to involve relevant support services in the development of new policies. He focuses on the outreach policy of special schools whereby teachers visit mainstream schools to offer support. However, he suggests that the failure to involve existing services in such new ventures can have serious consequences. At best the existing services may not support such development, while at worst, Muncey argues, they may undermine progress.

The City study

Coordination was seen as fundamental and central to the operation of CISS. This was how it differed from other services that dealt with fragments of the special needs jigsaw. CISS was to deliver a coherent, consistent and integrated approach to meeting requests for help. (As one head put it 'The idea of having one telephone number to call for help seemed a good idea'.) The idea was expressed by the Authority thus:

> The efficient direction and delivery of support services to schools requires a policy of co-ordination of *all the support services* which will...support schools in their catering for a wide range of individual needs...(our emphasis)

CISS was a central and focal point for consultation and initiation and, perhaps most important, was to be the *first* point for referrals.

All enquiries relating to special educational needs of children from schools or from parents (via schools or otherwise) would be directed to the CISS team *in the first instance.* In consultation with schools, parents and other relevant agencies (e.g. the District Health Authority or Social Services Directorate) a programme of response appropriate to the problem outlined in the enquiry would be drawn up. (our emphasis)

There were no guidelines laid down about what would happen after the first referral or indeed how CISS was going to set about organizing the other support services which, perhaps quite naturally, expressed concern that their autonomy and expertise may be compromised. During the consultation stage before CISS was set up the Service for the Hearing Impaired asked the following questions:

1. What would be the role of the heads of service and their relationships with CISS?
2. Should CISS be a purely administrative body (presumably passing on referrals according to an agreed formula)?
3. What will be the role of CISS in allocating the maximum levels of support – and if the maximum is exceeded then should the child be placed in a special school?

This was symptomatic of the concern that surrounded the concept of CISS – a body situated between the school and the special service that could interrupt rather than facilitate communication and the delivery of an efficient service. These anxieties were answered clearly and consistently with claims that CISS would make things better. The services would not expand but there would be more to go round because the service would be more efficiently operated by a central organization. The anxiety about the speed of response was answered simply – 'The CISS proposal will increase the response from support services'. CISS was simply going to make what already existed better by virtue of its administrative efficiency.

The relationship of CISS to other support services

One indicator of the level of interaction between CISS and other services is a comparison of the involvement of the services with schools prior to CISS inception and the degree to which CISS became part of that operation. Has CISS taken a central role in coordinating the relationship between schools and the other support services? And if CISS has not assumed a central role, what is it that CISS provides that makes it distinct and different?

CISS's level of involvement as a coordinating agency can be evaluated by looking at the numbers of pupils in contact with each of the specialist support services prior to the start of CISS. We have extrapolated from the number for the whole LEA to provide an estimate for the area covered by CISS (Table 5.1).

Table 5.1: Number of children receiving support from specialist services

Service for	LEA	Projected area*
Visually impaired children	138	34
Hearing impaired children	292	73
Physically impaired children	24	6

* Estimate of the number of children in CISS schools (based on the assumption that CISS schools have a representative sample of the school population of City LEA and arrived at by dividing the LEA figures by 4).

We can assume that some of these children will be attending special schools and that their needs in other areas of the curriculum will be met by the staff there, thus making CISS involvement unnecessary. Assuming that CISS has a quarter of these children in its catchment area, the figure for hearing impaired children could be reduced by 9 to around 64. The figure for visually impaired children would have to be reduced by a similar factor to arrive at the number of children who might require assistance in terms of special needs. It might be useful now to look at the results of interviews with the heads of other services, supplemented by additional interviews and data, to assess the involvement of CISS.

Service for the Visually Impaired

There had been 13 referrals from CISS. The involvement with CISS had been small for the following reasons:

- The children with a severe visual impairment were usually known to the service prior to joining school at five years (or earlier).
- There were few children in CISS schools who had a visual impairment – and very few of these had needed involvement from CISS.

CISS had a specific form for making referrals. None of the referrals proved to have had a profound visual impairment. Referrals via CISS tended to be from schools that had not already established a link with the Service for the Visually Impaired – where schools had established a link then the head simply contacted the service directly.

CISS had made three requests for INSET support from the Service for the Visually Impaired – one could not be met because of pressure from other schools. [The policy of the Service for the Visually Impaired is to provide INSET in schools (as a priority) where there is a child with visual impairment on the roll or where two or more schools have joined together.]

CISS and the Service for the Hearing Impaired

There had been six referrals from CISS but these all turned out to have normal hearing.

This service's arrangement is to inform CISS of their contact with hearing impaired children. If a referral is not felt to relate to their provision then they tell the head to contact CISS or the Psychological Service.

CISS had tended not to increase their involvement in a school if the Service for the Hearing Impaired was already involved with a particular child.

The head of service found that heads of mainstream schools take the 'immediate line' and contact the service directly rather than go through CISS. 'Why try something new if the old system is working?' There was initially great concern that CISS would 'take over' their area of provision, but the effect was felt to be minimal.

The Psychological Service

It is worth noting at the outset the comment of one member of the Psychological Service: that the contract was with the school directly and not with CISS. CISS and the Psychological Service were involved with the same schools and could work together, but the work was not coordinated by CISS in that CISS could in no way instruct educational psychologists in what their role should be.

> ...it was against our code of practice, our unions, our professional associations, to be responsible to a teacher for service delivery ...we wouldn't want to be responsible to a teacher because they have different disciplines, different structures.

In fact the reverse appeared to operate in many circumstances. The coordinator of CISS felt that educational psychologists were involved closely with establishing contracts with schools and directing the work of CISS personnel. They had been involved with a significant number of schools directly and were 'aware' of what was happening in all CISS schools.

With reference to the contract, the educational psychologist was adamant that the service was delivered to the CISS school and *not* to CISS itself as a central coordinating agency: 'I don't see that our time is available to the coordinator and CISS'. The contract wording was seen as critical: 'We invite X of the Psychological Service to liaise with us as part of his time...allocated to schools in the CISS project, *not to CISS*' (our emphasis).

We should not be surprised to find dissent within the discussion regarding appropriate roles for support services. As Dessent (1987) states:

> Special education is often an area in which territorial disputes can be rife. Thus, conflicts between different advisory and support staff, such as educational psychologists and advisers are commonplace. Such conflicts can lead to fruitless attemps to specify and delimit roles. (p. 165)

Muncey (1989) makes a similar point, stressing the need for established services to be involved in the planning of new services, which occurred in City LEA.

The relationship with the Psychological Service was seen by the CISS coordinator as one of the most positive developments that had occurred within the project. However, there was a need for clarification in the following areas:

- The role that each plays when going to provide assistance.
- Referral procedure – who decides who does what and when.
- Job descriptions and the division of labour – CISS personnel may be involved with the delivery of a joint INSET package with certain members of the service. Is parity possible (or desirable) in terms of the planning and delivery of the INSET?
- When is it best to work together and when is it desirable to work separately?

Coordination or collaboration?

The 'specialness' of CISS was due to its role as an organizer and coordinator of the other services so that the response to a request from a school was met with a coherent and well planned scheme of action. When the participants in the postal questionnaire were asked about the level of coordination that they had received, a far higher percentage of respondents from CISS schools (45 per cent) said that they had not received this form of help than the non-CISS respondents (28 per cent). This is a rather surprising finding, in contrast to that which one would expect given the statement of what CISS would *actually* do. It could be, of course, that the teachers in CISS schools had a completely different idea of what coordination is compared with the non-CISS teachers; perhaps the CISS respondents' expectations had been raised by the prelaunch publicity and contact with CISS staff to such an extent that the figure indicates a much higher level of disappointment.

Similarly when the Service for the Visually Impaired received six referrals on average per week, is it likely that these had arrived via CISS? It is difficult to resist the conclusion that was prompted by the head of service, that CISS has made a minimal effect on the organization and delivery of their service and that their fears of being 'taken over' by another layer of bureaucracy were unfounded. Similarly the Psychological Service could be seen to be defending their professional autonomy and freedom to act in a way that appeared to have little to do with CISS as coordinator, although there was good professional collaboration.

There was evidence to support CISS's role as a source of information about, if not a coordinator of, support services. It would appear that where a head is new to the authority then CISS acted as a very useful reference point from which to glean information about the support services that were available – the most positive head in the interviews held when CISS was a year old had only been in the authority for a short period. Not only did the service compare favourably with that which was available in the previous authority but it provided information about where to go and who to ask. But is this role of information giver a temporary one or will there always be a need for a group of people who know the 'system' and can direct people to help?

But what is coordination? Providing information – as in this case? Assuming responsibility for a concern and bringing resources to bear on it? Providing guidelines for action that the head might take and then letting the head work through the possibilities? Being a sounding board for ideas?

The *Chambers Dictionary* gives as one of its definitions of coordination: 'combining or integrating harmoniously'. Implicit in this definition is the idea of acting on the elements of a system so that they work together. This suggests that allowing the parts to function without intervention may not be sufficient; certainly permitting them to go on as they had done in the past was not what the originators of the plan had in mind. The plan suggested that the system could work more efficiently, which implies changes – thus if the various agencies have retained their previous work practices then this would appear to indicate that they have not been coordinated.

The LEA's original plan proposed that the amount of help and the speed of assistance could be increased by the role of a central coordinating agency. From evidence presented by heads of services and the survey of teachers within schools, there appeared to be little evidence that significant change had taken place.

One possible reason for this is that CISS had not been correctly accredited for 'facilitating' that which it had actually brought about. Be that as it may, to a significant proportion of respondents in CISS schools, the service is another agency that assists with special needs and has yet to establish itself, within their perceptions, as the hub of a wheel of support services.

This immediately poses the question: was it necessary for CISS to play the role of coordinator? If most heads continued to go directly to the service that they wanted then what role could CISS play? If CISS did not become involved in those cases where the children had sensory impairment does this imply that they were concerned mostly with children with learning and emotional difficulties? If this is the case, have they become a sort of up-dated Remedial Teaching Service?

Conclusions

In this chapter we have focused on the process of coordination. We suggest that as special needs provision has developed it has become more varied and hence more complex. To ensure optimal service delivery there should be a coordinated approach. But what is the reality?

Classroom level

The study by Gipps *et al.* (1987) raises questions about the extent of successful classroom liaison between class teachers and visiting support teachers. Although they found good practice, they also report examples of poor liaison and hence uncoordinated delivery of teaching to the children. Such instances were usually related to a lack of time, or to the poor use of the time available to meet, plan and monitor.

Service level

In the City study we found problems with coordination at the level of the support services. The issue of coordination had been recognized at the planning stage by the new special needs support service CISS and this had been designated as one of its main roles. In practice, however, two problems arose.

Firstly, it became obvious that for some children there was no need for such coordination. The established services for children with sensory and physical impairment had already developed clear links with schools. Neither the schools nor these services saw CISS as an aid to avoid duplication or inefficiency. On the contrary, it was seen as a possible bureaucratic hurdle standing in the way of a smooth-running system. This perspective was also taken by CISS itself.

In this example, however, we must remember that these children require particularly specialized services. For example, teachers of hearing impaired children are expected to have taken an extra qualification. In other instances, for children with the more prevalent mild or moderate learning difficulties, or behaviour difficulties, the new service worked well. All such children could be considered, within the context of their schools, and a service approach made. Compare this with a model current in another LEA we have examined where support teachers have only a loose affiliation to a general support service, and are also on the staff of, and work out from, particular kinds of special school. This approach may have the benefits of helping the teachers maintain links with a home base, for sharing ideas, etc., but duplication of effort is not uncommon. It is not unknown in this LEA for several different support teachers to be visiting the same schools, even occasionally the same child, as heads make full use of any extra assistance available.

The second issue concerns inter-service relationships. This can reveal itself in several ways but is particularly prevalent as a problem when a new service is being established. Almost inevitably this is a time when established services feel under threat. In City LEA, the new service was clearly designed to replace an established peripatetic remedial service, and also some special school provision. Existing staff could be appointed to the new service and their strengths could be utilized as the example has shown. However, a tension still arose.

A further tension was seen to arise in our study between the new support service, staffed by teachers, and the Psychological Service. Here there was an issue of professional identity, and primacy. In practice the two services worked well together, but the processes could best be described as collaboration, not coordination by one or the other. This is not a new phenomenon. Indeed, the Department of Education and Science published guidance in the 1970s when the then new procedures for the assessment of special educational needs were changing from a largely medical to a psycho-educational emphasis (GB.DES, 1975).

Implications for good practice

What we have shown is that there is a need for the coordination of service delivery *but* that this needs to be very carefully arranged if it is to succeed. At the level of the authority there is a need to coordinate the whole special needs provision at a macro, policy level. The development of a policy based upon a clear educational philosophy is necessary.

At the level of services, however, the need is to ensure coordination by good practice in collaboration between the services – which include special needs support, the Psychological Service, special schools and facilities – and the administration. Furthermore, these educational services must also collaborate well with health and social services and, of course, with the parents.

At the level of the school, there is again a need for a school policy. The 'whole-school approach' to special educational needs is frequently mentioned and arguments for its usefulness have been provided by Dessent (1987) and others. The school must find a way of coordinating both its own resources, and those from outside. The development of teachers as coordinators for special educational needs within schools has been a positive step in this direction.

Thus, in our view, the coordination of provision must be seen as a multi-level activity, differing in character at each level. It should *not* result in another layer of bureaucracy. Indeed it is best conceptualized as a *process*, not as a job requirement for one particular service. The aim is to maximize the development of collaboration between professionals and parents, and the efficient use of resources, for the purpose of delivering a comprehensive education to the children concerned.

Chapter 6
Contracts for Change

The problem was, you see, that the [Remedial Teaching Service] was giving us a good service *in their terms* – rather like the [Educational Psychology Service], there was not much wrong with what they offered in itself. But you see it wasn't what *we* wanted ...it was very frustrating. (Head, City Middle School)

Schools frequently complain not only that what is on offer from support services does not meet the school's specific requirements, but that there is very little – if any – discussion after an intervention; there is seldom any evaluation mechanism built into what support services do, and schools may be left feeling frustrated if not sometimes a little bitter about what has happened. As a result, neither the school nor the support agency learns much about itself, its partner or their relationship.

Clearly a greater degree of mutual accountability is called for: schools need to know in advance what is on offer, how it will be delivered, how it will be evaluated and what the likely effects will be. Similarly, support services must know exactly what a school is asking for and what their expectations are, and in the light of this information they should be able to plan sensitively. Ideally, all these processes should take place within an agreed and recognizable framework that – in the best sense – makes the partners accountable to each other.

As mentioned in Chapter 3, given the composition of the CISS Study Group it is not surprising that a contracting system with schools emerged as an important pillar of the CISS system; contracts have been considered in the practice of educational psychology for many years, and in certain areas of the psychologist's work – such as intervention in behaviour problems – they are by no means unusual.

However, the application of a contracting framework to the work of a support service is unusual. This chapter discusses some of the issues which lie behind both the principle and the actual adoption by CISS of a contracting system with schools; it illustrates some features of CISS contracts in practice; and finally it raises some questions about the system.

Aims and Backgrounds

In any social context, contracts are about agreed undertakings and the terms of those agreements. In their 'hardest' applications, contracts may carry penalties with them; in colloquial use, the idea of a contract is more to do with good will and reasonable professional expectations. The contract in CISS practice has a number of functions which subtend its use but which in sum suggest an operational coherence rather than a strictly accountable set of procedures. It will be clear from the illustrations below that – though in no way legally enforceable – this implicitly understood idea of a contract was taken very seriously indeed by schools and CISS alike.

The contract being central to the support project highlights the essence of the LEA's Plan for Special Educational Needs: the aim to produce a new simplified, more efficient support system that is enhanced by a process clearly indicating the ways in which inter-dependence between previously separated organizations was to develop.

Early in the planning, it was envisaged that contracts would initially run for a short period (say, a term or less); they would then be reviewed systematically and developed in the light of a joint evaluation. This idea of setting short-term objectives and regularly evaluating them expresses – again derived from the plan – an essentially strategic approach to meeting special needs; the steps are:

- identify and prioritize needs;
- develop plans;
- implement plans;
- evaluate progress.

The process is of course circular, since the last stage leads logically and practically to the reappraisal and prioritization of needs at the first stage.

In itself, this is no more than a common sense approach which breaks down larger issues into smaller, manageable chunks. (Of course, such an institutionalized process runs the risk of the breaking down process becoming an end in itself: the fundamental aims may become obscured, trivialized, even lost in the general milieu of day-to-day organizational pressures.)

Format

The contracts did not have a standard format, but took the form of a fairly ordinary letter. A number of the earlier contracts did not even mention the notion as such, though – significantly – subsequent communications and reviews referred to contracts. In the early stages of the project, there was a deliberate avoidance of over-standardization at any level in order to reconize the great variety in schools' organization and needs. After some time, all contracts were headed as contracts and given a reference number. This introduced an element of standardization and simultaneously reinforced the idea of formal, organizational relationships between CISS and the schools.

The actual contracts varied greatly in the way they were written; some were easily read and understood, the language clear and concise; others were more obscure, often giving a statement of general aims rather than definite short-term objectives underlying proposed action plans. Clearly it took some time for CISS workers to familiarize themselves with this new way of working, and it is not surprising that some early examples reflect uncertainty and lack of direction.

Negotiation of Contracts

The negotiation of contracts between CISS and the project schools raised many issues. It is possible that some of the early negotiation was undermined by the lack of clear publicity about CISS's role and the unpopularity of the basic information gathering process in some schools (see Chapter 4). Not surprisingly, the ease of negotiating depended on the particular context and the professionals involved: in some schools the whole process was easy because there was a clear perceived need and/or a clear perceived role for CISS to play; in other schools the negotiations were more difficult because they had to go through an unavoidable stage of clarifying roles and expectations as well as clarifying and planning input.

In the early days of the project, an agreed negotiating protocol dictated that senior CISS staff had to take part in the negotiations and, in certain circumstances, were required to check and confirm the subsequent contracts. On the school side heads were normally involved, with input from interested staff in some cases. Occasionally heads would devolve negotiation to other staff, though – whoever negotiated – protocol seemed to demand that contract and review letters were always addressed to the head.

Negotiation, therefore, can be seen at both an organizational level and at a more personal level. In a few of its most institutionalized forms, it was a case of senior staff deciding how people lower down in the hierarchy should work; at the more personal level, on the other hand, colleagues frequently decided how they themselves would work together. However, whatever the level of negotiation, success would depend on individuals working together and organizational support – though success in terms of personal relationships would not necessarily be judged in the same way as organizational success.

Contracts in Operation: Two Sketches of Practice

By way of illustration, two outlines of actual practice are presented. Although each one is unique, they are nevertheless broadly typical of the patterns of negotiation and interaction which occurred in the early days of CISS's operation. The reports reflect correspondence data on CISS files, though all the names used in this account are fictitious.

Sketch A: Bramall Lane Upper School

Although the basic information gathering forms were completed by the CISS assistant coordinator with the head of the school, the subsequent CISS input into the school was largely under the aegis of the deputy head. Protocol demanded that all the contracts and letters be sent to the head but she appeared to have had no active involvement with CISS otherwise.

The contract letters reveal that the CISS input had actually been a dual responsibility and activity. Both the assistant coordinator and the senior support teacher had letters on file with reviews of and plans for their respective activities. A brief résumé of the main correspondence follows.

2nd April. A letter from the senior support teacher indicating that as a result of meeting the special needs coordinator, it has been decided that the initial CISS support will be for two girls in their maths and English lessons. (It was discovered later that these two girls had been the subject of a request to the Remedial Teaching Service. CISS had subsequently assumed responsibility for this request.) The essence of this support is to be structured observation followed by the planning of appropriate 'small-step' programmes.

14th July. This letter from the assistant coordinator summarizes involvement in a paired-reading project in the school. It indicates that this project was instigated as a result of meetings as early as January when the deputy head and special needs coordinator were 'expressing a desire' to have a paired-reading project in the school. The assistant coordinator, along with another assistant coordinator, helped with some planning and preparation sessions during February after which they withdrew and the school personnel put the project into practice. The letter ends with an offer of assistance if a future project is planned. The involvement in the project was not 'contracted' in an earlier letter. This letter seems to have been written as the result of the assistant coordinator receiving a report from the special needs coordinator about the project, which appears to have been very successful.

28th July. This letter from the senior support teacher bears the title 'contract review' and refers to the earlier letter of 2nd April. The contents of the latter are now referred to as an 'agreed contract'. Most of the observation work appears to have been done in maths lessons. This has led to developments in record-keeping and a reported desire in the maths department to involve CISS in future resource development. The letter also mentions the possibility of a further paired-reading project next term (also mentioned above in the letter from the assistant coordinator), and the possibility of the LEA's computer division helping with the development of a computer-based SEN record-keeping system.

The letter ends with a request for the head to consider which areas mentioned should have priority and indicates that the school's priorities will be discussed with the deputy head early next term.

5th October. The senior support teacher writes that the paired-reading project has been prioritized. Already the senior support teacher and assistant coordinator have held one training session and another will be held shortly. Although not entitled a contract, this letter is later referred to as being such.

15th December. This letter from the assistant coordinator describes a meeting that both herself and the school's educational psychologist had with the support team. The outcome was another meeting in which the issue of record-keeping, and, in particular, a joint approach towards both pastoral and SEN records, was investigated. As a result of this meeting, the assistant coordinator and the educational psychologist now intend to spend some time working in the humanities area of the curriculum in order to help produce 'in-class records that are available for use by both subject and support teachers and which would have the function of both identifying and attempting to meet pupils' needs and also of informing teaching methodology and materials'.

18th December. Two days after the previous letter was written, the senior support teacher wrote this contract review letter. It refers to the letter of 5th October as being a 'contract' and describes the senior support teacher's and assistant coordinator's involvement with the paired-reading project during the term.

11th February. This is a letter with a contract title from a new senior support teacher who has now taken over from the previous one. It indicates that she is having regular meetings with the whole of the support team with a view towards planning future CISS involvement. It also adds that the planned record-keeping work involving the assistant coordinator and educational psychologist has had to be postponed because the chosen classes would be taken for most of the term by a student on teaching practice.

Sketch B: John Street Nursery School

All the correspondence between CISS and the school has involved one senior support teacher and the head. Their initial relationship evolved during the completion of the basic information gathering form and it subsequently developed with CISS involvement in the school. The contracts manifest a large degree of CISS involvement both in supporting individual children and in raising staff awareness of how to identify and meet special needs.

2nd March. This initial letter does not bear the 'contract' title but it is contractual in nature. It reflects the outcome of a discussion the senior support teacher had with the head. The letter reveals three strands of CISS input.

(1) There is to be involvement in making an informal assessment of a girl who is causing concern. There is to be the provision of a checklist and there is the comment that working with this girl will, hopefully, lead to a wider examination and development of 'record-keeping, identification of special educational needs and developing individual programmes'. Dates and times are given for the regular, weekly visits the senior support teacher will make. There is also a tentative review date.

(2) A date is given when the senior support teacher, plus an assistant coordinator, will attend a staff meeting to outline CISS philosophy and practice.

(3) An invitation is given for the staff to attend a meeting in another nursery when the senior support teacher, an assistant coordinator and an educational psychologist will talk about the requirements of the 1981 Education Act (GB.DES, 1981).

28th April. This is a review letter, though again not entitled as such. It refers to coming to the end of the 'first agreement'. It has apparently been written before a formal review meeting has been held. Mention is made of resources provided to help with curriculum-based assessment and record-keeping. No mention is made of the girl named in the earlier contract letter, though discussions with her teacher about general recording issues are referred to. A date is fixed for a formal review meeting and a request is made that time is provided to specifically consider the system devised thus far for recording special educational needs. The head is also requested to inform all the staff, at a staff meeting, about CISS's operations within the school so far.

18th June. This letter is entitled 'CISS Contract'. It indicates that the senior support teacher is still involved with the girl mentioned in the initial contract letter. Language has been identified as a priority area and three dates/times are given when the senior support teacher will visit to continue with assessing and meeting the girl's needs. A review date is also offered.

6th July. This is not an official review letter as such. It refers to a meeting involving the girl's teacher, the senior support teacher and staff from the first school which the girl is about to attend. Although it is confirmed that her present teacher's records will be passed on, there is no reference to any continuing CISS involvement with the girl. (Later the deputy head was to make some criticisms about the apparent lack of continuing support.) The impending review meeting is again mentioned.

28th September. This letter is an invitation for the staff to attend a series of INSET meetings organized by the senior support teacher and the head from another nursery school. These five meetings will each feature someone from an outside support service (SPS, health education, speech therapy, for example) to talk on the general theme of 'screening for special educational needs'. This letter is included because it represents a part of CISS's INSET input into the school.

29th September. This letter confirms the CISS contract for the autumn term. A support teacher will be visiting the school once a week throughout most of the term 'to support staff with the assessment of special educational needs and in the devising of practical approaches to classroom intervention'. During her period of involvement she will work with all three class teachers for a time. The senior support teacher now appears to be dropping out of active involvement in the school, though she still indicates a wish to visit the school. This contract is the result of a meeting between the senior support teacher, the support teacher and the head, held a few days previously. Although this contract naturally succeeds the first, it now appears the latter was never formally reviewed as the senior support teacher was ill and the planned meeting was cancelled.

18th December. This is a review letter outlining the results of a review meeting held the day before. The support teacher has worked with two class teachers, the third class having been taken mainly this term by supply staff. This work has involved preparatory work, in-class activities with individuals and groups and she has spent time talking with the teachers about individual children.

The letter also contains points about observing and identifying special needs. One reference concerns the use of resources seen at the INSET provided for all the nursery schools (see letter dated 29th September). A second reference concerns the early identification of special educational needs. There seems to be some conflict here (later confirmed in the interviews), as the senior support teacher noted comments made by the head indicating the difficulty and questioning the appropriateness of identifying apparent special needs as soon as a child enters the school.

9th February. This letter forms the contract for the spring term. The main thrust of the involvement will be the close observation of children to identify special educational needs. The observation will be based on ten-minute periods of close monitoring. To support and facilitate this monitoring, a new support teacher will visit the school once a week for a 75-minute session. Also an advisory teacher (at the behest of the adviser) will provide support by visiting the school for four of the afternoon sessions. There will be staff discussions after the support sessions which will be attended by the senior support teacher.

Perceptions of the Contracting System

Interviews with CISS and school staff revealed the contract system to be generally popular. The popularity lay in the fact that the contracts clearly defined the role and subsequent input of CISS staff; schools saw this as a clear resource commitment.

There were, of course, some concerns about the contracting system. Using the term 'contract' itself sometimes caused unease; such a term and concept seemed inappropriate in schools. (This opinion was tempered on occasion by the feeling that the idea of contracting was becoming prevalent in education and would have to be accommodated!) One senior teacher in a school felt that the contract system was more important to CISS than to him; he felt very strongly that the whole process of negotiation was invalid if it did not include *everyone* involved in the support process within the school.

Criticisms of contracting from the CISS members themselves centred largely on the time taken in writing contracts and review letters. Some also felt that all CISS staff should be able to write contracts, not just those in more senior positions. Similarly, the point of insisting on contracts for all schools was questioned.

Discussion

At present the contract forms a written record of the negotiation process between CISS and a client school and provides a set of short-term objectives. The review of the contract gives written confirmation that these objectives have been completed over a set period of time. A contract for each school shows how CISS is involved: it is working at supporting the organizations involved, as was intended. The successful completion of contracts legitimizes CISS's role as an effective system.

But the contracts have a wider significance than merely being bureaucratic legitimizers. The organizational aspect of the contract brings one aspect into greater focus. If a means-end model of organizational operation is considered, then the contract could be viewed as one of the means – along with negotiation and input – that CISS uses to support a client school and begin the process of change where appropriate. This rational process model is in accord with the idea of short-term objectives, to be reviewed and modified as necessary. These objectives are not 'ends', however. According to the terms of the LEA's Plan for Special Educational Needs, the ends are less easily definable constructs, such as 'effective support', 'a consistent response' and 'a greater likelihood of change'. Success in achieving these ends is not so easily evaluated, particularly in the short-term. Similarly the organizations involved are of a dynamic nature, constantly changing in nature so that the ends that are sought may only be temporarily or partially achieved until some change takes place.

It is advantageous to link the means and ends together. They are all part of the same process, which is to bring about and maintain a philosophical climate reflecting the LEA's ideas about how special needs are best met. Following this model the contracts become a part of the negotiating process. They are not snapshots, indicating a particular situation at a certain time; they are rather milestones in a continuous relationship. Once they are reached they are immediately superseded by the next milestone on the journey. How one reaches that milestone becomes the aim of the negotiating process. Each milestone is a means towards reaching the next one as the relationship between CISS and the school develops. This evolutionary model may be constrained superficially if the participating personnel within CISS and the school change, but the actual relationship between the organizations will continue. The surface structures may alter but the essential structures will remain. The quality of the latter, however, must be founded on the relationships of the participants.

As the negotiating journey proceeds from milestone to milestone, the short-term aim in reaching each milestone helps to keep the two organizations glued together on a joint course, albeit for a limited, specified time. But adhesion is not enough if a support service is to be a powerful change agent, providing support for change in policy and practice to facilitate special needs provision effectively. No matter how strong the 'glue', to have greater effect it must have some permeating quality. Successful permeation is about individuals interacting with other individuals. This interpersonal aspect will now be considered.

The interpersonal aspect

Schools are dynamic places. By nature they are in a constant state of change and development. Staff at all levels of the hierarchy come and go as do individuals in the pupil population. Periods of apparent constancy may be followed by overt upheavals and rearrangements within the organization. Even on a daily basis they are prone to disruption because of staff absence. Support services do not, of course, have their own pupil population but they are susceptible to the same problems that a school has arising from the absence and movement of staff.

When a teacher from CISS – or a similar organization – goes into a school and negotiates an input, the contract reflects a mutual organizational commitment. It goes deeper, however, in that it also reflects the relationship that has been made between the negotiators. For the support service to provide meaningful support not only on a 'macro' level to the school as an organization, but also on a 'micro' level to individual teachers, personal relationships are of fundamental importance. Successful relationships are built on familiarity and constancy. The term 'contract' and the organizational protocol requiring its production may seem to counter the personal aspect indicated above, but the short-term nature of contracts does facilitate personnel change at negotiator level without too much organizational disruption. It would be much more difficult, however, to compensate for the loss of a relationship that goes beyond organizational bonding and is based firmly on mutual understanding, respect and consequent affection. If the nature of schools means that they are constantly at organizational risk from staff absence and movement, then the support service will need to be constructed so that it can sustain some constancy of support to compensate for the turmoil of school life.

Organizational hierarchies

A final consideration about the negotiation of contracts is the effect of organizational hierarchies on the procedure. Because of their nature, hierarchies filter power downwards. Where power is devolved and delegated, there is still the need for upward referral for final approval. The greater the organizational effect any decision will have, the greater the necessity for executive approval. As we have noted, the role of a support service may increasingly be concerned with the change of attitudes and the development of appropriate procedures. These are fundamental aspects of school life and so the head's approval will be a prerequisite for any change to be considered. Ideas and directives may become diluted and altered as they are passed down the hierarchy for implementation. This is particularly the case when those implementing the decisions are unhappy because they have not been adequately consulted and they may be faced with more work. These are the people facing the daily reality of the school's organizational turmoil, bringing with it personal and logistical stresses. Whilst contracts often contain the names of others involved in negotiation and subsequent input, protocol demands that contracts pass between senior organizational figures and reflects their relationship, when the success or failure of CISS's input actually depends on the relationship of others involved in the organizational link. There is a danger, therefore, that the contracts may be seen as reflecting executive decisions that require implementation by others. If these 'others' have not been involved in the decision-making process then this may well be detrimental to the success of the organizational relationship. Similarly a lack of prior consultation may lead to contract reviews being seen as an appraisal of the teachers actively involved, rather than an overall appraisal of the effectiveness of the support process.

Conclusion

Drawing a final conclusion on the contract system is difficult. Contracts may provide a framework for organizational relationships to develop, but their continuance may reflect a desire for the relationships to remain at a formal organizational level; one organization would support another with the contract reinforcing the professional/client relationship. This would be acceptable if the prevailing philosophy is that special educational needs are essentially met by the input of outside experts. Many support services – including CISS – insist, however, on an essentially *enabling* philosophy and pedigree. In this case the role of the support service may be to develop a more informal relationship with schools based on personal relationships and commitment. The whole-school approach requires a philosophical commitment, and this is unlikely to come via a hierarchical diktat. The culture of a school is changed via personal interaction and example, so the prevailing aim has to be to develop the powerful informal relationships within the wider inter-organizational framework. Relying on the contract system to promote change could conceivably – and paradoxically – enable schools to keep support services at arm's length by restricting their input within controllable parameters.

This chapter was part-authored by Paul Geldeart.

Chapter 7
Providing INSET

The menu of activities developed by many support services now includes:

- withdrawal to regular sessions;
- individual teaching programmes/materials;
- assistance in the classroom;
- advice/INSET for school staff.

None of these items is new, but some LEAs have placed a new and different emphasis on certain items according to how SEN policy has been developed within the authority; as noted in Chapter 3, the support service often finds itself at the cutting edge of new developments, and although a suite of alternatives may be on offer, one or more items will usually be emphasized as these reflect particular aspects of policy which the LEA wishes to develop. Of these items, the one which marks the *biggest* break with tradition – and which may directly provide a means of dissemination of policy shifts – is INSET. As Gipps *et al.* (1987) observe, INSET 'can be a way of communicating to teachers what the LEA policy is, and why they have chosen it. It is explaining their side of the deal with teachers' (p. 89).

Some forms of INSET have often been available through the support services, but in the past these were typically limited to short, skills-based packages, frequently delivered after school hours to a volunteer audience organized through advisory or teacher centre programmes. Alternatively, support services typically gave assistance to educational psychologists; for example, in the delivery of programmes originated by school psychological services.

The emergence of INSET as a particularly important platform of support service activity, and as an expression of LEA policy, embodies three related principles:

- It deliberately moves the locus of intervention in difficulties from the individual student to his or her teacher; INSET is generally aimed at giving teachers themselves the skills to meet the individual needs and problems in their classes.
- In so doing, it reinforces the view of learning difficulties as the responsibility of all – not merely of specialist teachers and external services, but of every teacher in every classroom.
- Equally it brings attention to bear on the wider context of learning in which difficulties appear, and on how those difficulties may be closely correlated with wider aspects of curriculum and school organization.

These principles are clear expressions of the spirit and ideology of the Warnock Report (GB.DES, 1978) and the 1981 legislation (GB.DES, 1981) which carry – at least implicitly – a recognition that changes to the *structure* of special education must be accompanied, if not actually realized, by positive action on its *culture*; at its simplest, this means teaching appropriate understandings and attitudes – in addition to skills – within the whole educational community. This is clearly an enormous task, and one which increasingly falls to the advisory and, more particularly, the support services.

Some INSET programmes initiated by, or through, support services are designed as LEA-wide initiatives which deliver the same, single programme to all schools, regardless of the particular local need and situation. These programmes are essentially 'cascade' designs which deliver a centrally identified core of ideas serially through the various levels of organization. One such programme described by Gipps *et al.* (1987) in their study of six LEAs' arrangements for the support of children with SEN is that of Newtown, 'a medium sized city in the Midlands'. Newtown's programme of support concentrates on four areas: information giving, INSET, materials and 'advice and help'. The INSET programme (with its aim to make 'every teacher a teacher of children with special needs') is described thus:

> courses are run for SEN co-ordinators and then by them back at school to increase teachers' skill in developing and implementing

programmes for children with special needs. A major aspect of the in-service training involves practical application of the theoretical ideas put forward on the course for dealing with problems arising in the classroom. Once the co-ordinator has attended the course, he/she is then responsible for making his/her colleagues back at school aware of their responsibilities towards children with special needs in their classrooms. (pp. 59–60)

Thus the revised framework of INSET includes not only the more traditional skills-based packages (for example the special needs action programme (SNAP); Ainscow and Muncey, 1984), but increasingly a number of programmes aimed at instilling sympathetic attitudes as a prerequisite of more palpable change. These programmes may range from those explicitly concerned with 'raising consciousness' or awareness; through slightly more specific designs – concerned, say, with classroom and/or behaviour management – which are nevertheless more ideology-led than technically based; to those addressing the whole staff establishment on principles such as 'the whole-school approach' and the introduction of sympathetic in-school support systems. The particular menu, its targetted clients, and system and site of delivery will clearly vary from one LEA to another, reflecting both LEA policy and available resources within the team. In principle at least, it should also vary from school to school as needs are identified specific to particular situations.

Schools' Responses to INSET

If a greater emphasis on INSET represents a new arena of practice for the support services, it is no less a novelty for their client schools. Given their traditional dependence on the 'ambulance' model with its commonly understood roles and expectations, the schools might be expected to react uneasily to a system which first excuses itself of the responsibility for meeting individual needs, and then charges the schools themselves with those responsibilities. The study by Gipps *et al.* (1987) bears this out; within the six LEAs under study, of the 254 teachers asked to rank five options on the best way to help children with special needs, the largest number (82) gave a rank ordering of 1 to 'Smaller classes so the class teacher can cope', whilst the smallest number (15) identified 'Advice/in-service training for class teachers' as the priority. The average ranks (in order of preference) across the whole sample of 254 teachers are given in Table 7.1.

Table 7.1: Average ranks across the sample of 254 teachers

Option	Average rank
Smaller classes so the class teacher can cope	2.46
Withdrawal to regular sessions	2.61
Individual teaching programmes/materials	2.76
Assistance in the classroom	2.94
Advice/in-service training for class teachers	3.70

Source: Gipps *et al*. (1987, p. 81).

Clearly the significance of such a low attributed status for advice/INSET must be understood within the whole sample of LEAs, four of which had hardly any INSET provision. Yet even in Newtown, with its emphasis on – and targetted resourcing of – INSET as a key instrument of policy realization, the response is still not overenthusiastic. Of the sample of 34 Newtown teachers only four ranked advice/in-service training for teachers as the best way to help class teachers. Of course, the data of Gipps *et al*. do not permit us to separate 'advice' from INSET. (This is perhaps a weakness of their instrument, and hence their interpretation, for clearly there is a large difference between even the most precise 'advice' given – usually by one team member – on specific occasions, and a programme of clearly identifiable INSET, often delivered as a team effort.) Nevertheless, the cited complaints about INSET are common enough: class teachers complain of the lack of *practical* suggestions from courses, of difficulties of location and access, of the credibility of the course providers and so on.

However, it does remain that a generally more positive response is recorded for Newtown, and this may be partially explained in terms of, firstly, the recruitment of school staff themselves as course providers and secondly, the school-based nature of the courses. These features – implying as they do the idea of partnership and the importance of a school-focused programme – are of particular importance in the design and delivery of INSET within our case study service.

City Integration Support Service

The principle of negotiated support for schools is central to the organization of CISS, as discussed in Chapter 2. The structure of this organization, its team and their mode of delivery reflect a commitment to the varied use of the most appropriate resources as perceived by the school and the support service *in consultation*. There are clear limits to what may be available from the service, just as – from the point of view of the service – requests from schools will be limited by their own perceptions of their organization and needs. Each has its separate agenda therefore, and the aim of CISS is to minimize the excess of demand over resource – with its attendant dissatisfaction – whilst putting into action the LEA's policy on SEN (see Chapter 6).

INSET was an important element of the support services offered to schools by CISS. The content varies from items on a menu, more or less fixed according to the collective strengths of the team – for example, courses on paired reading, or Datapac – to courses arranged on a more *ad hoc* basis for particular schools; these might include short awareness programmes on aspects of the 1981 Education Act, say, or introductions to behaviour management. Whatever the nature of the INSET decided on by the school and CISS, it was invariably provided on the school's premises, except in rare cases where INSET was provided for more than one school at the same time, when one of the schools involved provided the venue.

One year after the project had started, just under half of the 59 schools in the CISS project had been involved in some form of CISS-provided INSET, ranging from one short meeting to a series of meetings over four or five weeks. All the nursery schools, approximately half the first and upper schools, and one-third of the middle schools had had courses. Although the courses provided covered a wide range of areas within the special needs field, just over one-third of all courses focused on behaviour management. All the teachers who had participated in courses were asked for their views about the INSET that had been provided and these views are now discussed.

Views from the schools

We were interested in how teachers in the project schools felt about INSET being a major aspect of CISS's role, and Table 7.2 shows teachers' responses to a questionnaire item.

Table 7.2: Should providing INSET be a major part of CISS's role?

	Nursery (raw score)	First (%)	Middle (%)	Upper (%)
Yes	8/13	54	44	67
No	1/13	16	26	13
Not sure	4/13	28	30	20
No response	0	2	0	0

We found that overall 53 per cent of the sample of teachers thought that INSET should be a major aspect of the role, 28 per cent were not sure and 20 per cent thought that it should not be. Where staff were not sure many seemed to feel that they gained most from CISS support in the classroom and felt that a concentration on INSET might detract from this work.

The INSET provided by CISS was frequently the only school-based special needs training that had been provided for teachers, and few teachers had had any other training in this area. The quantity and quality was therefore of crucial importance to the authority's implementation of its policies. The team therefore aimed to provide INSET which focused on central issues for the desegregation of children with special needs, such as mixed ability teaching. Predictably such aims had to be mediated by the perceptions of schools regarding their own special needs INSET priorities and by the current expertise of the CISS team.

Involvement in planning INSET

Other research has indicated that the early involvement of heads and teachers is important in the implementation of change, and from interviews and group discussion the CISS team appeared to give this consideration high priority. This issue was, therefore, one we addressed in the survey. Over 80 per cent of heads reported that they had been involved in planning at a general level and a few had been involved in detailed planning. In the case of class teachers a very different picture emerged: approximately three-quarters had not been involved and the few that had tended to be deputy heads or special needs coordinators. The lack of involvement was felt particularly keenly by staff who appeared to have relevant expertise which was not utilized. In practice the partnership model seems to have been made apparent only in the relationship between the head (in nursery, first and middle schools) or the relevant member of the senior management team (in upper schools) and members of the CISS team, who decided whether the CISS team would provide INSET and what the nature of that INSET should be. The possibilities of partnership in learning between course leaders and participants does not seem to have been explored in any of the courses run at the time of the survey, and indeed most of the INSET provided for the CISS team did not follow this model.

Although most teachers felt uninvolved in the planning of INSET, most perceived the school as having generated their school-based INSET. Few teachers identified lack of involvement as a cause for dissatisfaction with the INSET they had experienced, but the few who did felt strongly about it.

The provision of INSET involving full and open consultation with staff in schools is likely to be potentially threatening for members of a new support service who are in the process of adjusting to new roles and developing new skills themselves. It is, therefore, not surprising if members of such a team elect to provide an established INSET block, or package, with a familiar content and format. Such INSET also provides the support service with opportunities to extend the INSET provision skills of its own team. Nevertheless, these advantages must be balanced against the disadvantages of providing INSET which is not directly geared to the needs of individual schools and which may then lead to resentment from teachers of the kind which is discussed later. At this stage in its development CISS focused on providing INSET for schools rather than on identifying the strengths and expertise of members of a school's staff and supporting them in developing a school-based and school-focused INSET programme. New services have to establish credibility and there was some feeling within the team that providing INSET was one way of establishing that they had something worthwhile to offer.

As so few teachers were involved in deciding on the content and process of the INSET they received we were particularly interested in what teachers felt about the success of INSET. We looked first at what teachers hoped to gain from INSET and classified these hopes in terms of whether they were broadly consistent with the aims as seen by the course providers. All the nursery teachers and a high proportion of teachers in first schools (84 per cent) had expectations in line with those of the course providers. In middle schools there was a similarly high agreement, but rather less agreement in upper schools (71 per cent). We then looked at how teachers rated the overall success of their INSET and their assessments are shown in Table 7.3 (because of the small numbers of nursery teachers, figures for them are not expressed as percentages).

Table 7.3: Class teachers' views on the success of INSET

	Nursery (raw score)	First (%)	Middle (%)	Upper (%)
Successful	6/9	32	27	21
Partly successful	2/9	42	45	43
Not really successful	2/9	26	28	36

The percentage of teachers who rated the INSET as successful is rather low given the high level of agreement about aims. However, over 70 per cent of respondents felt that if not wholly successful, their courses were successful to some extent. The majority of those who felt that the INSET had not really been successful were teachers whose aims seemed incompatible with the aims of the course provider. Where teachers said that their courses had been less than satisfactory their comments tended to focus on a lack of practicability, a desire for new ideas or for consultation. As is commonly the case with in-service courses, some teachers felt that the suggestions made by course providers were not realistic in the context of a busy classroom. They commented: 'Too many major problems were simply overlooked'; 'Didn't fully take into account the ordinary classroom pressures'; '[We needed] more practical examples of how to adapt the curriculum'.

There is some evidence that teachers attending INSET expect to get new ideas rather than to gain access to and utilize the knowledge that they already have. A few teachers felt that they had not got any new ideas from the INSET they took part in, and clearly felt that they should have done: 'It was full of platitudes'; 'Many staff felt insulted to be told to do what they had been doing for years'.

Teachers' views on the effectiveness of courses

Changes in attitudes

In the survey we used teachers' reported changes in their attitudes as indicators of the effectiveness of courses which had taken place over the previous 12 months (Table 7.4). Some courses would, therefore, have only just been completed, giving teachers little time to work through the implications of what had been learned in terms of attitude and little time to introduce changes in the classroom.

Table 7.4: The effects of INSET on teachers' attitudes

	Nursery (raw score)	First (%)	Middle (%)	Upper (%)
Did effect	5/13	45	32	47
Did not effect	6/13	50	66	53
No response (or didn't know)	2/13	5	2	0

On the whole rather more teachers felt that their attitudes had not been affected than thought that they had. The comments participants made about the changes they had noticed focused on increases in awareness and understanding, on the development of a more reflective approach, and more positive attitudes. Replies were fairly evenly divided between these categories. Some changes were directly related to the content of the course while others were more general in nature. Examples of the sorts of comments made by teachers are: 'I am much more aware of children's needs and my own response to this'; 'Gave insight into how children have to adapt'; '[Gave me] awareness of teacher's contribution to failure of children'. For others the effort involved in changing long-standing habits was felt strongly: 'I am trying to be much more positive in the classroom'. A few teachers were reassured by their INSET since it confirmed the appropriateness of the approaches they were already using, leading to them feeling less isolated. Similar effects of INSET courses have been reported in a number of studies (see Wigley, 1989).

Teachers' evaluations of the extent to which INSET affected what they did in the classroom are shown in Table 7.5.

Table 7.5: The effects of INSET on teachers' behaviour

	Nursery (raw score)	First (%)	Middle (%)	Upper (%)
Did effect	5/13	49	42	27
Did not effect	6/13	46	56	60
No response (or didn't know)	2/13	5	2	13

Changes in behaviour

As with attitudes, there were rather more teachers who felt that CISS INSET had not affected their behaviour than thought that it had. Considering the high number who felt that the content of the courses was relevant, the majority stating that their behaviour had not been affected points to the importance of factors other than relevance which affect the way teachers change following INSET. One important factor in this respect appears to be the consonance between the philosophy of the course and the teachers' own beliefs (Berman and McLaughlin, 1978; Wigley, 1989); and there was some indication of significant discrepancies between the views of the CISS team and those of the teachers they were working with, particularly in relation to the issue of responsibility for children with special needs. Some teachers felt that they were being blamed for the difficulties that children had, that they were being asked to take on extra responsibilities and that the strain on teachers was not given sufficient recognition. A few teachers made comments which showed a basic difference between their understanding of the 'causes' of special needs and the understandings prevalent amongst workers in the field, for example: '...these strategies may help but not solve the problem'; 'There was the assumption that changing teachers' attitudes is the most important thing and will solve everything'.

Comments about the nature of changes that had occurred predictably clustered into groups relating to the nature of the INSET undertaken: changes in managing classroom behaviour, recording, assessment and adapting work to suit a range of attainments.

Changes in the school generally

Over half the respondents in first schools and two-thirds of those in middle schools felt that courses had affected practice in the school as a

Table 7.6: Effects of INSET on the school generally

	Nursery (raw score)	First (%)	Middle (%)	Upper (%)
Did effect	4/13	56	66	13
Did not effect	7/13	38	30	80
No response (or didn't know)	2/13	6	4	7

whole; these teachers were less likely to perceive changes in themselves (Table 7.6). The opposite was the case in nurseries and upper schools, but in the latter the aim had been to influence specific departments rather than the school as a whole. The sorts of changes identified by teachers related to changes in how staff as a whole behaved as well as to attitude and cognitive changes, for example: 'We have better insight and understanding of children's needs'. It was rare for teachers to mention changes in pupils as evidence of the effectiveness of the INSET.

Views of heads
For the purposes of this chapter we have presented our findings for heads and class teachers together, but there were some areas where the views of heads were markedly different from those of the staff. In general, heads had more positive views on the effects of courses on teachers and on the school, 15 out of 18 saying that INSET had affected the school. The dissonance between their views and those of other staff in this respect is exemplified by one head's comment – 'Recording and monitoring and reviewing are now done on a more organized basis' – in a school where few teachers thought there had been change. As well as being more positive about the general effect of courses on their schools, heads were also more likely to perceive staff attitudes and behaviour as having changed than were staff themselves.

Conclusions

We have seen that in some authorities INSET has played a particularly important role in the dissemination of knowledge about the authority's policies and in the development of the skills which are critical to their implementation; this was true of City LEA in our study. Within this framework the role developed by CISS was negotiated with schools and influenced by the experience and developing skills of the team members in providing INSET, as well as the feedback they received directly from schools and through the work of the evaluation team.

The positive perceptions of heads about INSET may simply reflect their gratitude that some INSET relating to special needs was now being provided. This does, however, have implications for the support which is offered to staff who are in the process of changing their ways of working and the attitudes which underpin these changes. Whereas most heads felt that INSET had positively affected the attitudes of staff, under half the staff respondents reported a change in their attitudes. Over optimistic assumptions about the speed of attitude change and the restructuring of ways of working related to such changes may mean that the need for continued facilitation of change is not recognized and that structures for providing support are not developed.

A support service should, in practice, be able to provide such support through its ongoing links with the school and through its variety of work with the school. However, post-INSET support may easily be overlooked as support teachers direct their attention to the competing demands of other work in the school.

Our research highlights the lack of participation by staff in decisions about INSET and the failure of utilizing opportunities for trained staff in schools to share their skills with colleagues. Our experience indicates that this is a situation common to many schools in many authorities.

This chapter was part-authored by Veronica Wigley.

Chapter 8
Direct Teaching

The traditional approach to helping children identified as having special educational needs was to provide them with extra and/or different teaching. More recently, as we have argued in Chapter 1, there has been a move away from this provision of direct teaching, towards the development of systems which offer advice and support. These changes came about as a result of two main developments: a critique of the previous system and the professional standing and development of the newly installed services.

In this chapter we shall review the issue of direct teaching, as we term it, in more detail. We shall review its demise, the growth of 'support' as a replacement activity, and reappraise its current standing in the range of provision that can be made for children with special educational needs.

The Demise of the Remedial Teacher

Traditionally children with special educational needs were helped either in special schools and units or by small group or individual teaching in mainstream schools. (That is, assuming they received any extra help.) This approach has an appealing simplicity. In the case of special schools, the expertise is concentrated in one place to which children are delivered. Here they can benefit from the whole day's diet of a curriculum – its content and delivery – which will be appropriate to their needs.

In the case of mainstream schools, a similar system applies. Children could be helped either full-time in special classes (or bottom streams), or could have the benefits of a mainstream curriculum for much of the time, supplemented by specific help, usually with literacy.

Unfortunately this superficially attractive system was found to have a number of flaws. Firstly, it is assumed that children's needs can be met by one of a very small number of different structural arrangements (special school, special class, withdrawal group). To be fair, it was also argued that these arrangements were means whereby the delivery of a special, expert service could be made.

But this brings us to the second flaw. In practice such a special service, in the sense of being expert and, by implication, superior, did not necessarily exist. For example, the Warnock Report (GB.DES, 1978) reported that only 25 per cent of teachers in special schools had extra qualifications in the teaching of children with special needs – and most of these were teachers of children with sensory impairments, where such a qualification was a requirement. The situation in mainstream schools was even less impressive. Here the typical remedial teacher at primary level was a part-time member of staff, with no training. Withdrawal groups might be found in the most unlikely and least attractive places (Moseley, 1974).

Thirdly, there was no guarantee that the curriculum content would be any different from that provided in the mainstream class or school – except that it might be 'watered down' or progress was more leisurely. There were, of course, interesting and, at least at the time, exciting developments. The work of Frostig on visual perception (see Frostig and Horne, 1964) and Kirk and his colleagues on language (see Kirk and Kirk, 1971) provided new curriculum materials and approaches based upon interesting ideas about children's problems. In the UK, the work of Tansley (1967) was particularly influential. However, these new developments were slow to make their mark in general remedial education. Their impact, rather, was on the new breed of remedial teachers who wished to undertake specialist training, which was developing in the late 1960s and 1970s, and on educational psychologists who had been trained at this time or earlier.

The fourth concern was of the amount of progress made by the children. Several studies in the 1960s in the UK showed that children receiving remedial education, usually in remedial centres, usually made good progress while receiving help, but that this 'washed out' once the assistance was removed and the children were back in their mainstream school without extra help (see Collins, 1961; Cashdan and Pumfrey, 1969). Thus, even if the teaching the children received had a positive effect at the time, how could it be ensured that this continued to be the case? Why did the host mainstream school not carry on the good work?

Fifthly, the 1970s saw a major challenge to the labels allocated to children with educational difficulties. The disquiet that had been growing at that time found full expression in the Warnock Report (GB.DES, 1978). Here, a clear critique of the old distinctions between 'remedial', 'slow learners' and a host of other labels was presented. Although the Warnock Committee's favoured replacement – special educational needs – is not without criticism, it does, by its pervasiveness, reinforce the need to be wary of false distinctions in terms of the underlying problem. Rather, the emphasis subsequently was on the action necessary to help the child. The problem with the previous system was exemplified by the common finding among practitioners that some of the children in remedial provision in mainstream schools could easily be 'swapped' for others in special schools for children with learning difficulties (ESN(M) schools as they were called).

Sixthly, there was the issue of efficiency. Comparisons were made between the numbers of children that could be helped by direct teaching and other methods. For example, one teacher could help a class of, say, 20 full-time, or perhaps 50, 60, 100, . . . part-time. The inescapable logic of this hid, of course, the question of what the child actually received. What was the optimal 'dose'?

The Growth of the Remedial Specialist

These, and other concerns, together with new positive developments led to a reappraisal of remedial and special education, as the two branches were then called.

Firstly, as mentioned above, there were new developments in teaching in the 1970s which looked very promising. These were indeed different from traditional practice and so required special training or study to extend teachers' skills.

Many LEAs approached this task by supporting teachers who undertook advanced qualifications. A number of courses were developed during the 1960s and 1970s and produced a new breed of specialist teacher. These teachers were imbued with both new skills and new ideas and ideologies. The new methods were taken up by many.

But how could these new ideas best be implemented? The other concerns, for example about carry-over effects, led to the need for the greater education of ordinary class or subject teachers in mainstream schools. The Pyramid selling model – popular, then infamous, in the early 1970s – was taken up. From the new breed of specialists were drawn advisers. Thus, while some returned to schools to implement change in their own settings, others took on a wider task.

This development was given a boost by the Warnock Report which recommended the development of teams of support teachers – special education advisory and support services. As Gipps *et al.* (1987) have shown, LEAs took this suggestion on board and over the next five to ten years there was a major expansion of such services.

These services varied in their remits. Some were similar to the earlier intiatives – essentially peripatetic teams of teachers taking groups of children, but possibly also advising other teachers, or contributing to some INSET. At the other end of the continuum, such services might be designated a major role in INSET and providing advice and support within school, with the direct teaching of children being relatively more limited. An example of the latter is the City Integration Support Service (CISS).

These developments also coincided with the general move towards more integration of children with a wide range of special educational needs. The advisory and support functions could then be applied relative to this variety of children, rather than an apparently narrower band of remedial children.

There were also examples of this new practice described in the literature. The main journals in this area (*Remedial Education*, in particular, and *Special Education: Forward Trends*) carried many papers describing variants of the support and advisory functions that could be undertaken, as opposed to direct teaching. Examples were given, for example, of teachers in secondary schools working with subject specialists to develop curriculum materials which were accessible to the pupils. In this example, the remedial, or special needs, teacher becomes a co-worker providing a special needs dimension to inform the subject specialist. Together, it was suggested, they could provide a better arrangement for the pupil in mainstream classes.

Also, this approach was recommended as being better than the remedial or special needs teacher working alone, to develop basic literacy skills. This new approach had relevance and, importantly, could raise the status of the teacher. No longer was he or she marginalized; now they were working as equals with other teachers, or even as superior specialists, particularly if they were based outside schools in support teams.

Mills (1988) provides an interesting study of special needs provision in 26 secondary schools in one LEA. This study shows the range of roles now undertaken by special needs staff in the schools. However, there was a lack of clarity with regard to the roles of the heads of departments interviewed. They no longer saw themselves as remedial teachers, but 'the schools with a clear, working job description were in the minority' (p. 21). Eight different types of support function provided by the special needs departments were found. Withdrawal was the most favoured type of organization, but support was also very popular – 20 schools reported this happened to some degree, and 22 departments considered they had advisory/liaison functions.

These new developments, therefore, also had the effect of increasing the standing of special needs specialists, both within schools and by the formation of LEA support teacher teams. A by-product of this development was that the advisory role had a perceived higher status than the direct teaching role. This largely reflected the real change in status that accompanied these role shifts. However, this perhaps led to a tendency to develop this role more, with a consequent diminution of the resources allocated to direct teaching.

The CISS Study

When CISS was set up it was determined that it should not be simply a peripatetic teaching service; rather its range of activities should be much broader (see Chapter 2). However, the direct teaching of children with special educational needs was seen as one of the three major tasks, the others being to give advice on children with SEN and to provide INSET. How, then, did this plan work out over the first two years or so of the implementation of CISS?

The beginning

Our interviews with key officers and elected members of the staff of CISS revealed a variety of views on the question of direct teaching.

Some were concerned that CISS should not be 'another advisory service', to quote one interviewee. However, it was recognized that CISS should differ from the Remedial Teaching Service (RTS) which it superseded. Thus a *balance* between direct teaching and advisory and support work was envisaged, but with the former being relatively reduced compared with the RTS.

However, our interviewees recognized the problems that such a change in emphasis might cause. As one said: 'Is CISS going to come in and actually provide an individual programme of work for that child, or is it simply going to tell me how to do it – even though I haven't got the time to do it?' A similar point was made by another interviewee who, while referring to psychologists, raised an important concern about support generally: '...a psychologist who drops in for half a day a week and talks about eight children, but never in fact sees any of them, is not in the school's mind doing the job that they are paid for'.

Thus, as CISS was getting underway, there were ideological concerns about its emphasis which centred on the distinction between work which was hands-on, direct teaching of children or providing materials and programmes, contrasted with advice and support. Not surprisingly, perhaps, there was a worry that the former either would diminish, or not develop; but there is also the more subtle suspicion felt about provision which is not direct, hands-on.

The first two terms

We interviewed heads after half a term and special needs coordinators (SENCs) during the second term of CISS.

The heads' views on CISS were affected at this stage by their concern at the amount of information being asked of them (see Chapter 4). However, the heads also expressed their views on what they saw as the benefits to be gained by CISS. Interestingly, there was a difference between the first and middle school heads. Three-quarters of the first school heads wanted help in the classroom, in the direct teaching of children alongside the class teacher, whereas this was the case with only one in five middle school heads, who rather favoured the idea of INSET and advice.

This raises the important issue of the *developmental stage* of the child. We found a difference in the types of support requested by heads of schools with children at two different stages in their education. Underlying this is the fact that children in first schools are at a stage when they are attempting to learn basic skills and build up a fundamental knowledge. They are also, in maturity terms, less able in general to be able to plan their own work and development, use resources independently and generalize strategies.

Our interviews with the 24 SENCs during the second term revealed a significant minority reporting what was seen as *loss of support*. Eight interviewees reported that during the first term of CISS they had lost direct teaching support. In three cases this did not matter too much as the children had improved, but the other five were concerned about the loss.

This factor was perhaps inevitable when one service is replaced by another, but it was aggravated here by the time taken in learning about the school rather than providing support (see Chapter 4). CISS was also operating at about half-strength at this time.

By the second term, however, 9 of the 24 schools had received in-class support of work with individual children – 18 in all. Of the nine SENCs for these schools, six were at least satisfied and three dissatisfied with what was provided. Why was this? To delve further we also sought the views of the class teachers concerned.

The general picture was of children looking forward to and enjoying the work they did with the support teacher, and making progress. In most of the schools the support teacher had been working with the target child as a member of a larger group and had not been withdrawing the child for individual help. Eight of the nine schools had been able to implement joint planning sessions between the class and support teachers, which also allowed more general discussion and advice to be exchanged. Overall, eight of the nine class teachers were satisfied with the provision being made.

Returning to the SENCs we find other agendas. Those SENCs who were dissatisfied raised several concerns. Two were disappointed with the *amount* of help received. However, in both schools, in-class support was being provided for four children for half a day a week, and had been so for about six weeks at the time of interview. No school was receiving more, and two of the satisfied SENCs were receiving less. Also, the provision of direct teaching in the two schools where the SENCs were dissatisfied over the amount was slightly *more* than before the start of CISS, the SENCs told us. Why, then, should there be dissatisfaction?

One of these five SENCs considered that half a day a week was totally inadequate to make any impression on the school's needs. The second felt let down that CISS had promised so much and her expectations had not been fulfilled.

The third SENC who was dissatisfied expressed disappointment not with quantity but with the nature of what was offered – it was not what she had asked for. This was, in fact, a rather special situation. She had spent a once-weekly session throughout the previous year in a special school improving her expertise with SEN. She had hoped the support teacher would cover her to allow this to continue.

After two terms, therefore, we find that CISS is providing direct support for children with SEN, and that this varies across schools. Where this was provided the class teachers were satisfied, but there was less satisfaction among SENCs. The dissatisfactions varied from the particular concerns of one teacher for her own in-service development, to the belief that the amount of provision was insufficient. Also, there was a concern that the provision made did not match that promised in the publicity material, or at least in terms of how this material was interpreted by the teacher.

The longer term

We surveyed a large number of schools that had either had CISS for four terms or had carried on with their previous provision. Overall, 351 CISS and 303 non-CISS heads and teachers were surveyed (see Chapter 11 for details). In general, there were few significant differences between the two groups (CISS and non-CISS) in terms of the quality or quantity of support they had received; this was also the case for direct teaching. Overall, there was great dissatisfaction with the *quantity* of provision, but some, though limited, satisfaction with quality (Table 8.1).

Only 41 per cent of the teachers surveyed considered the quality of direct teaching of children with SEN to be acceptable or better, and only 21 per cent considered it to be of sufficient quantity. This result was similar for both services. Where they did differ was in the types of alternative provision that CISS intended to make. With respect to both quantity and quality CISS was rated significantly better for providing INSET, assisting with policy-making regarding SEN and providing advice on classroom management. However, the reason for

Table 8.1: Percentage of CISS and non-CISS respondents rating direct teaching for quality and quantity ($N = 684$)

	Very poor or poor	Acceptable	Very good or good
Quality	59	25	16
Quantity	80	16	5

the difference was the greater dissatisfaction of the non-CISS teachers with the service provided in these three areas. Those rating the CISS service acceptable or better were only 43, 47 and 34 per cent, for quantity and 50, 53 and 42 per cent for quality, respectively.

After seven terms

In our final trawl of consumer opinion we surveyed by questionnaire the heads and SENCs of all the CISS schools (54 and 39, respectively – in some smaller schools there was no SENC, the head took this role and three SENCs were absent with long-term illnesses). There was a 92 per cent response rate – very high for a postal survey, with equivalent rates from each group (50 heads, 36 SENCs).

Once again we sought consumers' views on the service provided. In Table 8.2 we provide the results of this exercise, and have included the rating for all the types of provision offered, not only direct teaching.

The first point to make is that 93 per cent of the respondents had received direct teaching in their schools, and this was therefore the most common type of provision. Educational programmes (84 per cent) and INSET (74 per cent) had also been provided to a large number of schools.

The quality of the input was generally considered to be at least acceptable. For direct teaching this judgement was reported by 87 per cent of respondents. However, the *quantity* of help provided was not considered satisfactory for direct teaching, only about half (52 per cent) considered this adequate or better. These low levels of satisfaction with quantity were also true of other areas. The comments made by the heads and SENCs made it clear that their criticisms were due to lack of resources, not the input of CISS *per se*.

Table 8.2: Heads' and special needs coordinators' views on the quantity and quality of CISS after seven terms ($N = 86$)

Aspect of service	Respondents receiving service (%)	Quality – respondents rating acceptable or good (%)	Quantity – respondents rating adequate (%)
Direct teaching	93	87	52
Devising educational programmes	84	87	56
INSET	76	94	66
Providing teaching material	64	78	50
Advice on managing behaviour	60	75	61
Coordinating help	58	82	73
Assistance with SEN policy	52	84	82
Advice on classroom management	45	95	61
Support for change	26	92	65

The heads and SENCs were also asked to identify and prioritize the help they would like from CISS in the future, using the same five types of provision listed in earlier questionnaires (see Chapter 7). Overall, the most popular kind of support was assistance in the classroom (see Table 8.3) and this was closely followed by a preference for smaller classes. Interestingly, regular withdrawal was the least favoured option. This result can be compared with the earlier views of the larger sample of teachers after four terms (compared with the later sample of heads and SENCs).

Both samples gave priority to assistance in the classroom and smaller classes. However, withdrawal was an option more favoured by the earlier sample. Teachers in CISS schools at that time, after four terms, also gave priority to assistance in class, with smaller classes next. However, withdrawal was a more favoured option in the earlier survey with 33 per cent of respondents placing it first or second choice compared with only six per cent of the later sample.

Table 8.3: Heads' and special needs coordinators' rankings for support

	Ranking					Un-placed	Average ranking	Final ranking
	1	2	3	4	5			
Regular withdrawal	5	4	4	12	25	32	4	5
Individual teaching programme	19	21	23	13	1	7	2.43	3
Assistance in classroom	50	15	25	3	1	3	2.15	1
Advice and/or INSET	24	9	23	11	9	8	2.63	4
Smaller classes	30	4	12	13	4	20	2.28	2

Some Conclusions from the City Study

Our study of City LEA has revealed some interesting information concerning the place of direct teaching. The original remit for CISS included this as one of three major forms of provision, but by including the other two (INSET and giving advice on children) the authority was making a clear statement – it was shifting the emphasis away from direct teaching to a three-way approach. This was due to the general shift in opinion nationally about appropriate provision, which we reviewed earlier in this chapter, and the commitment of the authority to a service which gave a high priority to integrating children, and therefore required support also to be integrated.

Our study provides a developmental perspective, over nearly two and a half years, on this change, gauging the opinions primarily of teachers (heads, SENCs and class teachers) and also the initial perspective of policy-makers and senior officers. We can see a shift in the opinions of teachers over this period. Initially there was concern that the changes would lead to a loss of resources: the teacher who takes a child for direct teaching is a clear resource, the support teacher offering advice or INSET is not always seen as such. Even where teachers had sympathy for the concept of integration, they were concerned that the new service, CISS, was integration on the cheap. For example, when we met with the LEA's committee of all teacher associations at the start of CISS, one representative made the telling comment: 'The LEA has its hand on its heart when it's speaking but never seems to get it into its trouser pocket...'.

There was also the concern that the new service might even be a hidden form of resource reduction. The early days, however, revealed that the range of provision promised would be made and, in particular, direct teaching was offered. However, the way that CISS was started up did lead to a limited service which to some schools was a real loss. The service was not fully staffed and spent a significant amount of time collecting information (see also Chapter 4). This reinforced the fears of some.

However, once underway, there was increased satisfaction with the service. Direct teaching was seen as helpful, and was indeed being provided in over 90 per cent of the schools. There was still a concern about quantity, but quality was considered generally satisfactory (although there was still room for improvement). But the teachers in City LEA, unlike for example those in the six LEAs surveyed by Gipps *et al.* (1987), were less keen on direct teaching being provided in a withdrawal situation. They wanted support in the classroom and this was the method favoured by the CISS team.

Direct Teaching: A Wider perspective

In this chapter we have traced the development of in-school support. There has been a change in view among advisers, psychologists and support staff, suggesting that direct teaching, particularly by withdrawing children individually, should be replaced by a support service which is advisory and supportive. This view has its origins in both a critique of practice and a development of professional identity. This has been a general shift and, during the 1980s, many LEAs developed advisory and support services, and tended to downgrade or fade out services where direct teaching was the major function.

But is this the way forward? To answer this question we will consider two main issues. Firstly, we must consider the extent to which the views of educationists, advisers, psychologists and others compared with those at the chalk face – teachers, heads and special needs coordinators, who are of course themselves teachers or heads. Secondly, we must analyse the model of provision promulgated and match this against children's needs.

Advisers versus teachers?

There is no doubt in our minds that teachers generally welcome extra support, and particularly that which they perceive as 'real'. In practice this means resources such as equipment or teacher time. Teachers who have seen these types of resources removed tend to see them as a real loss, even if other forms of support are provided. Unfortunately, the alternative provision favoured by those not in schools has been seen by teachers as less relevant. Advice and support, therefore, have often been compared unfavourably with what they replaced, because there was a loss of what was perceived to be a 'real' resource, such as direct teaching.

This is not, of course, surprising. Yet in many LEAs this change has occurred leading to dissatisfaction with the new system. Our study of one LEA's introduction of a new system has shown these tensions, but has also shown that the new service need not forsake direct teaching. What was changed with the introduction of the CISS team was the relative emphasis on direct teaching and its location, changes which had begun in the later work of the Remedial Teaching Service, but which were now formalized and publicly stated. Here, teachers could still gain direct support for children either through limited support teacher time, or from the use of support assistants (see Chapter 9). Thus the new service was able to broaden its range of resources on offer, and to undertake work which was in keeping with a belief in integration: direct support generally was provided in class. This is not to say that the teachers were all satisfied. We have seen how there were still concerns, particularly with the amount of help available. However, there was an increasingly positive view about what was being offered.

In City LEA this process took about two years. During this time the INSET provided was also important. Here teachers were introduced to the LEA's philosophy and also given some knowledge and skills relevant to their own professional development. Thus it was possible to integrate, to some extent, the different strands of the new system, its philosophy and practical consequences.

Children's needs versus ideology?

The concerns about direct teaching as a form of support have several foundations. The first relates to integration. Withdrawing children to individual or small group work can be seen as segregating (removal to special schools, of course, is even more so). Withdrawal by another teacher may also remove the responsibility for the child's learning in key areas – reading is taught by the special needs teacher, not the class teacher. Withdrawal also, in practice, tends to remove the child from the mainstream curriculum, at least for part of the time. In secondary schools in particular this can lead to a knock-on effect where the child misses one set of lessons which then interferes with learning in another. Direct teaching is also expensive, particularly if it is on an individual basis. There is also evidence to question the long-term usefulness of such withdrawal, special group teaching, and whether it is indeed 'special'.

But do these concerns necessarily lead to a view that direct teaching is inappropriate? Although the shift away from direct teaching to support and advice has become the new orthodoxy, we suggest this needs to be re-examined.

1. Location

A major criticism with the earlier system of direct teaching concerned location. It was often carried out in poor surroundings on a withdrawal basis. But this is not inevitable. As we have shown in our review of City LEA, some services have developed support in the classroom. This allows, although it does not guarantee, other problems to be overcome. Teachers can collaborate, team-teach, and plan work jointly. The class teacher does not lose the responsibility for the child. Rather, this is retained, but the teacher has support in this. There are now various examples of this in operation. For example, hearing impaired youngsters integrated into the mainstream may well require in-class support to enable them to understand the language as well as the concepts being put across. Another LEA has developed integrated resources where children with a range of SEN are supported in class (with some withdrawal for specific purposes) with some positive results (Lindsay, 1989).

2. Type of support

A fundamental question concerns what actual support specific children need in order to learn and develop optimally. The hearing impaired child, for example, may require in-class support as described above, but may also benefit from some work specific to language development. Thus, whereas this youngster requires access to the same science curriculum, he or she may have a specific need for a different curriculum area or one at a lower level to match the disability. A child with a physical disability may not require any teacher support additional to that normally provided, but may need particular equipment, or help with toileting and self-care to be provided by a non-teaching support assistant.

A child with a major, intractable literacy problem may require full access to the mainstream curriculum, and may improve his or her literacy skills on such a programme, but is likely also to need specific help with literacy. This may require different materials from those used in mainstream lessons (such as simpler reading texts, specific groups of spellings). This situation may also require a particular teaching method which can only be carried out in a small group.

In fact the range of possible needs is large, and with any one child more than one type of provision is likely to be required. Consequently it is necessary to provide a variety of support. In our view, this menu must include:

- direct teaching;
- small group work;
- specialized curriculum content;
- teaching method;
- different schedules of feedback, correction and reinforcement;
- particular attention to ecological factors including distractions, size of class base, space.

Unfortunately, such an analysis is rarely conducted or its implications acted on. Even children for whom a statement is provided often end up with provision which takes account of only a small number of their needs.

Implications

The place of direct teaching in the range of provision LEAs and schools offer should be reappraised. In our view there is a real need for this to be available to children with SEN. This is not to deny the need for advisory and support services, or for INSET. These are also very necessary. Our point is that there has been a general shift away from one towards the other, whereas what is required is a balance between the two.

Chapter 9
Support Assistants

VERONICA WIGLEY

Extra help in classrooms is the sort of help teachers in CISS LEA schools would most like in order to meet the needs of all children (see Chapter 11). Hodgson, Clunies-Ross and Hegarty (1984) found that teachers saw non-teaching assistants as a major resource in integrating pupils. Such assistants are employed to carry out activities with children under the guidance of teachers. Although in some authorities peripatetic teachers give extra support to individual children, much of the support has been, and is likely to continue to be, provided by ancillary staff who are variously known as non-teaching assistants, support assistants and even in one school as 'pink ladies'.

Despite the importance attached to support assistant work there have, until recently, been few studies which have looked at this area. One of these (Robson, 1986) examined the role of support assistants in primary schools, on a county-wide basis. Robson concluded that support assistants should work with all the children in a group, rather than solely with the child designated for that help, and emphasized the need for training for both teachers and assistants. Later studies of support assistants in mainstream schools have explored the nature of the work assistants do and the sort of training they would like to receive (see Clayton, 1989a, b), and a few workers have explored approaches to training (Clayton, 1989a, b; Robson, 1990). Woolf and Bassett (1989) looked at the characteristics of assistants in special schools and at their relationships with teachers and children. Again the need for training was emphasized and the experience of assistants in this country was contrasted with that of their counterparts in the USA.

Little has been reported on the sort of help which teachers feel they are receiving, or on the nature of the help which they would like to receive. Little attention has been given to the implications of decisions about the nature and targetting of extra support in the classroom for the integration of children with special needs.

In this chapter we describe that part of the CISS study which provided information about the day-to-day work of support assistants in the context of their schools and LEA. The nature of support assistants' work from the perspectives of teachers and support assistants is described and related to LEA policy. Some issues relating to the utilization of non-professional workers in the classroom and integration are also discussed.

City LEA Support Assistants

The study was carried out approximately 18 months after the pilot project had been introduced into schools. At the time the authority employed three categories of support assistants. The vast majority were employed to support an individual child or a small group of children, for a specific number of hours, in a specified school. There were also CISS-based support assistants who supported a wide range of children with special needs and were employed for the full school day in schools or at another base, and assistants who were employed in special schools to help with general classroom duties as well as to support children. Some of these support assistants occasionally supported individual children in mainstream schools but such children would normally be on the roll of a special school.

This study gathered information about the first two of these categories from local authority records and documents, from a survey of staff working in schools which were taking part in the CISS project and from a sample of staff working in other mainstream schools in the authority. In addition three mini case studies were completed.

Questionnaires were administered to all support assistants in CISS schools and to a sample of support assistants in non-CISS schools who worked for 15 hours per week. This was the modal number of hours worked by all support assistants in the authority. The information gathered focused on: background information; the nature of the work carried out by support assistants from their own perspective and from that of class teachers and heads; how their work was directed; and views on training needs. In addition, questionnaires were sent to the class teachers in whose classrooms the support assistants worked, and heads were invited to comment on any aspect of the role of support assistants.

The response rate for support assistants in CISS schools was 71 per cent and was 73 per cent in non-CISS schools. The response rates from teachers were 76 and 72 per cent, respectively. Fourteen heads in schools where support assistants were surveyed replied to an invitation to give their views on the role of support assistants.

Three full-time support assistants were employed by the authority and worked from the project base. The work of these three was explored through short case studies to obtain a detailed picture of their work, which would not only be of value in itself but would also inform the development of the questionnaire designed for other support assistants. One of the evaluation team spent a day with each of the support assistants observing their work in three schools. Staff in these schools, who worked with the support assistants, were then interviewed on a separate occasion as was the head. The support assistants themselves were interviewed before and after the classroom observation sessions.

Characteristics of Support Assistants

All the support assistants employed at this time were women. The effects of recruitment policies were monitored by the authority in line with its equal opportunities policies, but it appeared that applications from men were rare. The number of workers from broad ethnic minority groups appeared to be in proportion to the size of these groups in the area.

Employment

Support assistants were employed on a temporary contract for a maximum of 27 hours per week. The number of hours worked could be increased or decreased at short notice. Although assistants were not paid for school holidays, wages were paid on a monthly basis throughout the year. These conditions of service and pay appeared to be similar to those in local authorities nearby, but there was some concern amongst support assistants and teachers, particularly heads, about the insecure nature of the employment.

About half the assistants were concerned about pay, their contract or lack of training. Some replies expressed concern about how the job was valued – 'I feel that the job is very much underestimated by the local education authorities. This is reflected in the wages they offer' – while one assistant pointed out that the nature of her contract meant that if she was successful with a child, progressively fewer hours were necessary, resulting in a reduction in wages.

'The contract we are given is a certain trap.... It has no security and no benefits... [respondent describes progressive reduction in her hours]... I can't quit because I would not be eligible to claim DHSS until 26 weeks after and they [the LEA] certainly wouldn't relieve me from my duties'.

One head felt particularly strongly about the issue of contracts;

'My main area of concern relates to the temporary nature of contracts... It makes sense that one should look towards an increasing measure of independence [of supported pupils]... Unfortunately this...means that...hours [can be] considerably reduced over a period of time and sometimes with very little warning... If we are to attract the quality and calibre required for a position which must have recognized status it is vital that ways and means are devised to offer sufficient hours of a permanent nature which will give the necessary security for the employee.'

Experience and training

The work background of support assistants was varied. Few had worked with children, although many had children of their own. Of the 20 support assistants in CISS schools only four had ever worked with children with special needs before. Five said that they had had some training but this varied widely from a quarter of an hour each week with a peripatetic teacher to a unit of a BEd course. A similar picture of little previous experience or training emerged for support assistants working in non-CISS schools. Support assistants commented: 'I could do the work better if I had been trained, even a short course would do or some sort of book pack', and another said: 'I really enjoy my work but would welcome any opportunity to expand my abilities to help the children'. Heads, too, expressed concern:

'Support assistants need training and when trained should be recognized by being paid a realistic rate'.

Workbase

There were far more support assistants working in first schools than in any other sector – approximately two-thirds of all those employed in mainstream schools. It appeared that many primary aged children who would previously have been in segregated education were now being supported in mainstream schools. There were very few older children in mainstream schools who received support, and this suggests that those who had previously been segregated were not being reintegrated at this stage. At the time of the study there were only five support assistants in all the upper schools of the authority.

Their clients

The 20 support assistants working in CISS schools who replied to the questionnaire worked with 16 boys and six girls. It is not possible to characterize the children in terms of their special needs because of the overlapping, changing nature of these needs.

The Nature of the Work Carried Out by Support Assistants in Classrooms

In this authority the support of a non-teaching assistant and the number of hours to be provided were specified in the statement as part of the educational provision. The support assistant was provided to meet the needs of a specific child.

Most assistants said that they worked with their children both individually and in groups. In this respect there were no clear differences between those who worked in CISS schools and those who did not. Observation and interviews with teachers indicated a general consensus that it was not useful to work only with individuals. It was felt that children saw themselves as different if they were the only ones to receive concentrated individual help and that such help was unfair since there were other children in the class with similar needs.

Such views reflect those of Dessent (1987), who has argued that the idea of a continuum of special needs implies a continuum of provision, and that providing specialist help for one child and not for another with broadly similar needs is not compatible with the concept of a continuum. The LEA's policy of allocating individually based support could therefore be seen as integrationist rather than non-segregationist, but in practice was mediated by the support assistants and by the teachers they worked with in the direction of non-segregation.

Assistants occasionally helped out in a general way in the classroom by mounting work or preparing materials for craft work, particularly in non-project schools. Only one support assistant reported that she sometimes helped with the class as a whole while the teacher worked with individual children or small groups of children with special needs. None of the teachers who were observed and interviewed had ever used the assistant in this way. It was much more usual for teachers to see the work of a support assistant with an individual or small group as 'freeing' them to work with the rest of the class.

The tasks undertaken

The majority of support assistants were employed to help children to benefit from the learning experiences offered, and/or to cope with social relationships in the classroom. A few were employed solely to care for children in a physical sense. Helping children to develop self-help skills was not mentioned at all by support assistants but was mentioned by a few teachers.

Both support assistants and teachers were asked to describe ways in which the support assistant helped in the classroom, and both identified a wide range of activities. Because this was an exploratory study participants were asked what support assistants did rather than given a checklist to tick off tasks. For this reason, the aspects of the role identified are likely to have been those which were salient to the respondent and are unlikely therefore to reflect the whole range of duties of any particular support assistant.

1. *Helping children with work*
The most frequent focus of responses from all support assistants and all teachers was helping children to cope with work in the classroom,

and included working alongside children, providing motivation and encouragement, and helping children to develop cognitive skills. Approximately two-thirds of the teachers and half the support assistants mentioned the cognitive aspects of the work. The help children received with language development (specifically in oral, reading, writing and spelling skills) was frequently mentioned by teachers but there were few references to carrying out a specific programme with a child.

Support assistants typically referred in general terms to what they did, for example: 'Work alongside the child to help him with his work'. Teachers were sometimes more explicit about the nature of the work, citing for example: 'Helps with the development of mathematical concepts... through games'; 'In science assists with reading, doing and recording experiments'. It was not at all clear from the questionnaires what support assistants actually did when they helped with, for example, reading, doing and recording or developing concepts. There appeared to be a general consensus amongst teachers and assistants that it was not the job of the support assistant to adapt materials. This was seen as part of the professional role of teachers. Nevertheless, it appeared from interviews with teachers that many provided material for the child. Observation of support assistants revealed that many of them orally translated the material so that children understood the content. Children were then helped through the process of completing the related tasks. This was done by providing further information, asking questions to help children to structure what they were doing and providing encouragement. Thus, in reality, support assistants were used as *teaching assistants* rather than as *non-teaching assistants*.

Very few teachers described these aspects of the support assistants' role in any detail, but interviews with teachers indicated that there was some concern. Whereas teachers felt that it was appropriate that physical care should be undertaken by assistants, reservations, in the interests of the child, were expressed by both class teachers and heads in relation to their role in helping to develop cognitive and social skills. Yet this was the very area in which support assistants in this authority appeared to be most closely involved. Although there is little information available at present about the varying roles of support assistants in different local authorities, it is clear that in some authorities they are employed only to carry out physical care.

2. *Helping with behaviour or emotional difficulties*

Another important aspect of the work centred on this area, which appeared to be more salient to teachers than to support assistants and was identified by just under half the project teachers and just over one-third of teachers not working in project schools. Teachers described the sorts of difficulties where support assistants helped, for example: 'Ready to intervene at the first sign of a temper tantrum or any kind of unsociable behaviour'; 'Aggressive behaviour towards adults and other children'; 'Disruptive behaviour, for example climbing over furniture, throwing things...'.

At least one support assistant saw her role in terms of 'Protecting other children from his violence', but more usually support assistants described what they did in terms of calming the child down when disturbances occurred or avoiding such events by keeping the child occupied. A few support assistants helped children with social development and described their work as involving 'Helping the child to become a member of the group'.

3. *Helping with sensory impairment*

Support for children with sensory difficulties was directed primarily towards those with impaired hearing, which was directly attributable to the fact that one of the schools in the project had an attached unit for children with a hearing impairment. Few support assistants, less than one-quarter, supported children who had physical difficulties.

The Supervision of Support Assistants' Work

Given the predominance of support assistants' help with children's work the nature and amount of professional supervision they received from teachers takes on a greater importance than it would if assistants were simply helping to meet physical needs, such as helping with toileting, helping children to change for PE. The importance teachers placed on directing support assistants' work and the extent to which they were able to carry this out were issues explored in the survey and in individual interviews with teachers.

All teachers said that they usually discussed the support assistant's work with her, and this was confirmed by the replies of support assistants. In addition, almost three-quarters of the assistants in CISS and non-CISS schools said that they discussed their work with someone else. In CISS schools this tended to be a visiting support teacher and in non-CISS schools one of the senior management team. Very few support assistants and very few teachers specified that they discussed the support assistant's work with the special educational needs coordinator in the school.

Case study data indicated that the CISS-based support assistants discussed their work, in particular monitoring, with the support teachers at their base, but received day-to-day instructions, which varied widely in quality, from the class or subject teacher.

Class teachers in CISS schools clearly felt that it was important to direct support assistants' work in terms of the content of what was taught (15 out of 18 thought that this was important rather than quite important or not important), but fewer attached equal importance to direction in terms of the teaching approach to be used. In non-CISS schools there were slightly more class teachers who felt that direction relating to the teaching approaches used was important than those who felt that direction in terms of what was taught was important. These differences are small and may be due to the differing nature of the difficulties dealt with by the support assistants.

At least a quarter of all the teachers usually gave no directions about how to approach specific tasks. Although in CISS schools half the teachers said that they normally stated what was to be done and how to go about it, one-quarter said that they only gave directions about what should be done and not about how to approach it, as did a slightly higher proportion of teachers in non-CISS schools. Whereas most of the teachers in CISS schools who felt it was important to give guidance about teaching methods did so, in non-CISS schools many teachers who felt that it was important to give this sort of guidance did not do so in practice.

The significance to be attached to the direction, or lack of it, of support assistant's help depends to a large extent on the previous training and experience of the assistant as well as on the nature of the help being given. The previous section outlined the lack of experience of most assistants in working with children with special needs. Concern about the nature of the direction and guidance teachers give to their assistants therefore appears to be well founded.

The three full-time support assistants based with CISS had all worked with children with special needs before and two of them had worked for many years in special schools. It was ironic that this was the group of assistants who were most closely supervised.

Although two-thirds of the teachers in CISS schools and about half those in non-CISS schools said that there was a specific time for discussing work with the support assistant, detailed replies indicated a less sanguine situation. Teachers reported that generally discussion took place just before the lesson began, in snatched moments before school, during breaktimes or at the end of a session. It is not possible from the questionnaires to assess the quality of this discussion but the case studies provided some evidence that not all teachers' directions about how to approach a task with a child were sufficiently detailed to enable even a support assistant with some experience to support a child appropriately.

The length of time for discussions between support assistants and class teachers varied considerably, ranging from 5 to 10 minutes daily to 30 minutes daily, and from 5 to 10 minutes weekly to 60 minutes weekly. Over half the support assistants in non-CISS schools were able to talk to the teacher for between 5 and 15 minutes each day, compared with one-fifth of those in CISS schools. Generally in CISS schools the emphasis appeared to be on discussion in blocks of time either on a daily or weekly basis. One support assistant clearly indicated that the hour she spent in discussion each week was in her own time; there is no information about how many other support assistants were having discussions in their own time.

Teachers in CISS schools were most concerned about the time that it took to prepare work for the support assistant to do with the child. Teachers in non-CISS schools recognized these difficulties.

The Contribution of Support Assistants to Non-segregation

Teachers unanimously agreed that the help of assistants was essential in maintaining the children they supported in mainstream schools. In addition, the vast majority of teachers felt that with this help the child who received support was appropriately placed in a mainstream school.

The benefits identified by teachers centred predictably on benefits to the individual specified child and included reference to the general help the child was able to receive in class, including extra help in curriculum areas, the help given to the child in clarifying the nature of the task and paying attention to the task, and the confidence the child gained from having support. Teachers also mentioned the progress the child made both academically and in terms of acceptance as a member of the class. A few teachers said that the presence of the support assistant enabled them to work individually with the child while the support assistant ensured that other children carried on with their work.

Heads were almost unanimous in feeling that support assistants provided valuable help. The following are typical comments:

> They can be very valuable and a great asset to child and class teacher, but suitability, including personality, are absolutely vital to a successful working relationship.

> Excellent to have someone to establish a close relationship with a child who has emotional problems... can be supportive to more than one child in group situations... Invaluable as an observer in monitoring situations.

Other benefits of having support assistants' help were seen as benefits for the class. Several heads pointed out that having a support assistant in the classroom was beneficial for other children in the class as well as the specified child. Teachers specifically mentioned that having a support assistant enabled them to concentrate on the rest of the class while the support assistant was working with the specified child, and that other children were able to work undisturbed if the assistant was there to prevent outbursts. Some teachers felt that other children in the class benefited if they were included in the group of children working with the support assistant. Generally teachers in CISS and non-CISS schools identified similar benefits. Although teachers valued the help they received, approximately half the CISS teachers and two-thirds of those in non-CISS schools felt that there were also some problems. These included lack of experience and training, the effect on children who felt 'different' because they had special help, and the effect on the class if they were unsure about the support assistant's role. Several teachers also voiced their concern about children with special needs being taught by unskilled assistants, and this was echoed by some heads. One felt that employing support assistants to work with children with learning difficulties was 'Like going back to the good old days when we gave the remedial class to the newest teacher'.

In the few cases where heads were not enthusiastic it appeared that there had been a difficult relationship between a particular support assistant and the school, or that the teacher resented having to spend time in preparation or that the head was unconvinced of the rationale for employing support assistants.

Several heads who were positive about the use of support assistants in other respects worried about the time taken for teachers to work effectively with a support assistant. One felt very strongly that the time the teacher spent on preparing work for the support assistant and directing her in how to use it would have been better spent if the teacher had worked with the child directly. Related to this comment was the feeling of another head that support assistants should be able to adapt academic work so that is was suitable for the child, because of the amount of teacher time that was involved if they were not able to do so. However, it was recognized that unless training was given this was probably an unrealistic expectation.

Conclusions

This study has revealed the important part that can be played by support assistants in helping children with special needs in main-stream classes. In the authority studied here, support assistants were working in both the area which was receiving support from the integration support service (CISS) and in the remaining three-quarters of the city, which was dependent on the traditional service. However, only three of the support assistants within the CISS schools were specifically linked to the team.

Support assistants played a significant role in the learning process of the children they supported, although there was some disagree-ment among teachers over the exact nature of this input. Support assistants were not 'child minders'. On the contrary, the teachers' expectations of them, which they fulfilled in many cases, put these staff at the forefront of facilitating the child's development. Yet in many cases the time available for teachers to discuss matters with the support assistant was very short.

The importance of support assistants has been recognized in the recently released draft DES Circular *Staffing for Pupils with Special Needs* (GB.DES, 1990). The DES prefers the description 'special support assistants' (SSAs). In their staffing model which 'should not be seen as a blueprint but as a broad guide for planning purposes' (para. 4), the DES suggests levels of both teacher and SSA support suitable for differing degrees of learning difficulty. For the present purposes it is interesting to note that SSAs are specifically referred to in relation to a range of children with special needs. In some cases it is suggested that there should be equivalent SSA and teacher support, but for the most profoundly and multihandicapped youngsters 50 per cent more SSA than teacher support is recommended. However, their general directions are more difficult to follow in integrated settings, and the DES urges a careful examination of the specific needs of the child in question.

The deployment of support assistants in classrooms may have an impact on the whole class. They can be used to release the teacher at specific times to carry out other work, or, by interacting with a group, can facilitate meaningful integration of the child with special educational needs into a wider community. This contribution can be subtle but nevertheless powerful. The experience of one of us (Geoff Lindsay) in one other large authority in particular suggests to us that the removal of general assistant help from primary classrooms, for financial reasons, has been a major factor contributing to an increase in the number of referrals for formal assessment under the 1981 Education Act (GB.DES, 1981). Schools have felt that their ability to cope with children with special needs has decreased to an unacceptable level following this reduction of help in the classroom. Our study of City LEA focused on support assistants who were specifically designated to work with particular children, but our research revealed that their influence and support could, and usually did, permeate more widely.

Chapter 10
City Integration Support Service in Action

The following case study represents a specific interpretation of the events that have taken place in one organizational situation (CISS); these interpretations are based on visits and interviews. Of course, when choosing a school for a final illustration of CISS's work, it soon became apparent that there was no such thing as a 'typical' example of CISS input. School staffs differ not only one from the other, but they also change frequently within themselves. Similarly CISS staff have individual strengths and skills. It becomes almost impossible, therefore, to look for the 'typical' example. However, we hope that this example will be sufficiently recognizable to most professionals who have had recent experiences of support services, and that it will provide some insights for further discussion. All names used are, of course, fictitious.

Stancliffe First School

Although there had been regular systematic support from CISS, the school itself had not had consistent leadership because the head had left after a period of illness. During this period she had been present at only some of the negotiations with CISS. When the school was visited in November, it was in the charge of an acting head, who was a deputy head in another school. The previous acting head had reverted to her English as a second language role within the school at her own request, since she was about to take early retirement.

Stancliffe First is an inner-city school. There are approximately 130 children on the roll and the majority of these come from Asian backgrounds. Most of the children live close to the school in terraced-house accommodation. The school population remains constant with little movement in and out of the immediate area. When a child changes address, its new one tends to be nearby so that there is no change of school for the child.

The constancy of the population is paralleled by the relative stability of the staff. The staffing of the school comprises the head plus 7.5 full-time equivalent teachers. There are two full-time nursery nurses and two part-time non-teaching assistants. Most of the staff have been at the school for some time and this has helped to maintain a feeling of normality despite the problems over the head's illness and subsequent departure.

The school is to move into a new, larger building within the next three years but at the moment it is housed in an old building surrounded by a playground on three sides. It is set among houses, shops and factories and near two very busy roads. Inside the school there are a variety of teaching areas and it is impossible to reach the head's room or the staffroom without going through at least one of these areas.

The school is bright and colourful inside, the walls covered with pictures and children's work. Many of the teaching areas have more than one adult working with the children and the benefits of a good staffing ratio are easily apparent.

The whole school appears as a busy place, with lots going on. It has taken part in local curriculum initiatives and generally the ethos reflects a comment of Mrs King's (the CISS worker): 'They're involved in quite a lot of things. They're not a backward, non-thinking type of school'.

The participants

For the purposes of this case study four people were interviewed: three people from the school – the present acting head, Mr Green; the past acting head, Miss Cooper; and the special needs coordinator (SENC), Mrs Fox – and from the CISS team Mrs King who had both negotiated the first contract and also carried out the support work in the school. (These names are pseudonyms devised to protect the anonymity of the actual staff concerned.)

Mrs King
Mrs King took up her appointment with CISS in February 1987. At the time of her introduction to Stancliffe, she was initially employed as a support teacher, though in September 1987 she was appointed to a senior support teacher's post. A CISS assistant coordinator had made the initial contact with the school over the telephone and accompanied Mrs King into the school on the first visit. All subsequent input was left to Mrs King, although normally a senior support teacher would have been responsible for negotiating the contract; Mrs King's negotiating role was thus a divergence from the normal protocol adopted by the CISS team. Prior to her working for CISS, Mrs King had worked both as an advisory teacher and in a special school.

Miss Cooper
Miss Cooper originally held a scale post for English as a second language. She had become the acting head when the head suffered a prolonged period of absence in hospital. The head returned to work but she was not fully fit and had to have further time off work before she eventually resigned from the post. These problems all coincided with the beginning of CISS. Consequently Miss Cooper was dealing with CISS much of the time as the acting head, though this was after the initial approaches and negotiations had taken place. She did, however, lead the school during the summer term when the negotiated input was taking place. After the summer Miss Cooper elected to revert to scale post teacher as she intended to retire at the end of that term.

Mrs Fox
Mrs Fox was the acting deputy head during the period that Miss Cooper was the acting head. Mrs Fox had become the SENC in the school, although she had originally held a post for maths development. She has remained a class teacher during the period of CISS's input.

Mr Green
Mr Green came to the school in September to be the acting head, having been deputy head in a nearby school. Although he took over the negotiations and general dealings with CISS in mid-stream, he was

familiar with its operation because his previous school had had some CISS input.

Previous support

Stancliffe First had received various types of support before CISS appeared. There had been some Remedial Teaching Service (RTS) input, though this had not been very recently. The school had also been supported by the Schools Psychological Service and the Advisory Service. One other type of support was from the Service for the Hearing Impaired, which supported one boy with input from a non-teaching assistant (NTA) for 15 hours per week. This NTA is overseen by a teacher from the school for the deaf, who visits twice a week.

The separate inputs from both the Advisory Service and the Service for the Hearing Impaired reflect the ideas behind the creation of CISS. Two Advisers ran a workshop on behaviour management, promoting a whole-school philosophy. The support from the Service for the Hearing Impaired continues to be very much classroom based, with the support teacher working alongside the class teacher. The staff generally seem to have been very happy with both these approaches and this is reflected in their specified needs in the basic information gathering form.

There has been less satisfaction with the RTS and the Schools Psychological Service. The RTS had been called in on occasions but their input was not perceived as being very useful:

> Also I...with things coming in from the RTS, was not always happy that the actual apparatus, you know reading materials, was in line with the sort of thing that we would be promoting... I felt that there was quite a dichotomy between the aims of what was going on in the mainstream of curriculum work and what the RTS was doing. (*Miss Cooper*)

> We had an occasional visit pre...before last year [from the RTS]...I think on the whole, those occasional visits, people didn't find them all that helpful. (*Miss Cooper*)

The Schools Psychological Service had been involved in the school but the feeling was very much that the educational psychologists had offered reassurance and wider perspectives but little tangible help: 'I feel some of these experts are very far removed from actual classroom teaching' (*Mrs Fox*). Similarly, communication problems have further made the staff less favourable in their attitude: 'we'd had problems with communications if you like. We'd refer our child, there'd be a long gap and then somebody would come in and then somebody else would come in . . . the RTS and the School Psychological Service' (*Mrs Fox*).

The result of their experience with previous support systems has been that the staff have tended to try to cope with learning difficulties themselves.

> What has happened . . . is that people have been thrown back on their own resources. When they've really felt that things that they've been left with for children to do, they've looked at those and sometimes . . . that's been helpful and sometimes not. And I think on the whole teachers have finished up deciding what *they* can do best. (*Miss Cooper*)

Again this attitude was reflected in the basic information gathering form, when the only specific child mentioned for help was the boy with the hearing problem who was already being supported:

> He was the only child that was mentioned to me . . . they cope automatically with any problems . . . For example I popped in at lunchtime today . . . one of the teachers was eating her dinner . . . I said, 'How are you doing?' . . . She said, 'Oh all right, we had a bit of a do last week . . . we got a girl in with no English at all . . . she's only been in the country three weeks'. Now some schools would have rung us immediately . . . What help is available? . . . Who's coming in? . . . What do we do with them? . . . They've [the staff] just taken it as part of . . . 'Who is this child?' . . . 'We have the resources to cope' . . . They haven't thought about ringing. So no children have ever been mentioned to me. So, therefore, whatever help they wanted from CISS wasn't in the area of individual children. It was in the area of helping them, the INSET. (*Mrs King*)

Early perceptions of CISS

In our interviews with the school staff, we explored their early perceptions of CISS's role. CISS's introduction to the school had suffered because of the then head's illness and consequent sporadic absence, and also because CISS had been unable to fill all its posts before starting work. Mrs King began visiting the school in March to negotiate the CISS input. An initial introduction to the school had been made by an assistant coordinator but the negotiations were left to Mrs King.

Both Miss Cooper and Mrs Fox expressed some early ignorance and misgivings about what CISS's role was to be:

> I don't think we realized the full implications of it. (*Miss Cooper*)

> It didn't turn out to be what I thought it was... Until I met Mrs King I'd a very vague idea of what [CISS] was all about. (*Mrs Fox*)

Although both these teachers had been aware of CISS's creation, they were not aware of its detailed role. Certainly it was seen as something akin to, but superior to, the RTS:

> What was a possibility that we could see, was a much more, much closer contact with the support service than we'd had previously with the RTS. (*Miss Cooper*)

> I feel that staff should have been more informed about it, about what it was about because I think most people thought like I did, that it was an RTS really. (*Mrs Fox*)

Certainly the head had felt wary about CISS and its role in school: 'Confidentially, we had problems with the head. She felt very threatened if anybody, what she called criticized. It was helpful criticism if you like, but she didn't take it like that' (*Mrs Fox*). The gatekeeping role of the head can considerably influence the effect that outside agencies can have in a school. If the head is cautious or antipathetic, then life can become very difficult for an outsider coming in. By controlling information, the head can affect perceptions of the staff: 'She [Mrs King] was [an outsider] at first, we were maybe wary of each other, I wasn't quite sure what her role would be' (*Mrs Fox*).

As will be seen later Mrs King overcame this obstacle and was very successful. Preparing a school for an innovation like CISS, which may affect the very foundations of the school's framework, is very important and should be done with care and planning. Where there is the possibility of executive influence blocking or manipulating the innovation, then strategies must be devised to overcome or by-pass it if possible. It would seem very risky to leave success at school level to an individual's negotiating skills and persistence. This micro level approach demands staff of extraordinary skill and resilience, not to say charisma!

To conclude this section it is worth briefly considering the feelings of Mr Green, the new acting head. When he arrived at Stancliffe First, he had already had some indirect experience of CISS at his previous school. CISS input there had involved supporting specific children, but none in his class. His initial experience at Stancliffe was not positive: 'When I first arrived, I was totally confused because I was dealing with three different people. . . . ' The reason for this was that in September 1987 internal staffing reorganization in CISS dictated the input of a new senior support teacher at Stancliffe. Therefore Mr Green met Mrs King, along with an assistant coordinator and the new senior support teacher. As Mr Green was a newcomer to the school and to dealing directly with CISS this was somewhat confusing. Ironically the senior support teacher did not actually have any input because she left CISS, and Mrs King's subsequent promotion to senior support teacher meant that the situation in the school did not change.

Mr Green was also unaware of CISS's wider role: 'I'd actually no idea that CISS were involved in INSET work'. This again raised the problem of effective prior publicity and information. Mr Green's early perceptions of CISS were based on a vague knowledge plus vicarious experience, neither very positive. His initial personal experience at Stancliffe was confusing and negative. Although he had subsequently been able to see the good work CISS had done and was still doing in the school, his early negative experiences left him with strong doubts, as will be seen.

The contract

Once Mrs King began visiting the school to complete the basic information gathering form, the contract began to evolve. Initial contact was with the then head but this was quickly followed by more extensive negotiations with Miss Cooper, who became acting head, and Mrs Fox, who was both acting deputy head and special educational needs coordinator. Miss Cooper was very particular that there was as much whole staff involvement as possible and so consultations were made at staff meetings.

As a result of general staff consultation and particular negotiations with Miss Cooper and Mrs Fox, a contract was finally sent to the school dated 8th June. This was two and a half months after Mrs King had begun visiting the school for the contract negotiations.

The contract has two main aspects. The first was the development of a record-keeping system for the school and the second was some INSET input from the teacher of the deaf who already visited the school. There was no mention of supporting any individual children at this stage. The contract period was to start on 16th June and be completed on 22nd June. On this latter date there was to be a staff meeting to review the work completed during the period.

After Mr Green came to the school in September, a new contract was negotiated. This was finally sent to Mr Green by Mrs King on 9th November. It would appear that the negotiations took a whole half term. Allowing for the fact that Mr Green was new to the school and would need some time to settle in, this would still be considered a long negotiating period. Part of the problem was that Mrs King could not organize the INSET required by the school. This was not the fault of Mrs King, but rather the result of too many demands being put on the sensory impairment services within the authority. Consequently Mrs King was to lead some INSET work herself on special needs identification. This was to consist of three fortnightly sessions with the whole staff at staff meetings. The first of these had taken place when we visited the school for the first time.

As with the first contract, the second contained no reference to supporting individual children.

The concept of contracts was discussed in the interviews. The quasi-legal aspect had coloured early perceptions:

> It [the contract idea] seemed odd to me. It seemed very legal and not the norm for a school . . . it seemed odd to me, it seemed out-of-place that it needed to be so formally done. (*Mrs Fox*)

> I'd heard of contracts but I didn't know exactly what they involved. And I presumed that they would be something much more complicated than . . . they are. (*Mr Green*)

Miss Cooper referred to the legal aspects of contracts – in particular their 'binding' nature – and indicated that she had doubts as to this aspect: '...is this letting us in for more than we had really bargained for? Are we taking on...more than we might need?' Certainly she felt that this style of contract negotiating was becoming a part of school life:

> It is cropping up in other areas, in the sense that when Mrs Black [Adviser] came to see us because we are pitifully short of reasonable equipment...it was made quite clear to us that we would not get it unless...in other words there is the beginning of perhaps negotiations all round. (*Miss Cooper*)

Mrs Fox, however, could see a more positive side to the contract: 'I think that perhaps it sets you a goal and so many weeks to accomplish it...it's a good thing is that. I think if you have a goal for a certain date, things do get done'. The impression given in the interviews was that the three teachers at Stancliffe had mixed feelings and concepts about the contract idea. Whilst they were not against having a short-term programme and goals based on their own perceived needs, they felt somewhat intimidated by the term 'contract'. Their early concerns may well have disappeared since they have seen how the CISS contract idea works.

Making a formal contract might be seen as irrelevant and even counterproductive considering the relative intimacy of Stancliffe First School in terms of both size and ethos. This impression is easy to acquire in hindsight, knowing that all the personalities involved developed very positive and affectionate relationships. Different personalities may not have worked so easily together, necessitating the formal commitment of a contract. The school could have a different head in the near future and, similarly, CISS could have a different support teacher in the school. In either case negotiating the contract may have a different perspective and importance. At least in Stancliffe there is now a tradition of positive contract negotiation and completion to be followed.

CISS input

During the interviews in Stancliffe it became clear that a major reason for CISS's positive acceptance in the school was the interpersonal skills of Mrs King: 'What's gone on in this school so far has been successful and it's down to personalities. Mrs King is a very nice person, a very approachable person' (*Mr Green*). In her initial contacts with the school Mrs King had gained much admiration for the way she had dealt with the head before the latter had become ill and had to leave:

> Mrs King was super in that she was very, very tactful . . . she knew just how to handle it. I thought there might be some hassle because you see the head had originally done the school records herself . . . I don't know how she did it, but she did it beautifully, we didn't have any hassle at all. (*Mrs Fox*).

This ability to be both reassuring and willing to listen has meant she has not been perceived as a threat to anyone's professional ability: 'I think we've been particularly lucky with [Mrs King] because . . . she is a person who is not a threat to people, she is very supportive and helpful and open to suggestion' (*Mrs Fox*).

She has responded to the welcoming atmosphere in the school by becoming a part of the life of the school: ' . . . everybody knows her and she's very much greeted as one of the family when she comes' (*Mrs Fox*). The staff at Stancliffe have been told by Mrs King why she enjoys visiting the school: 'She knows all the staff by first name . . . she says, I'm not so uptight when I come in here because I know people are knowing we're not going to offer any instant solutions' (*Mrs Fox*).

Mrs King has brought to the school more than pleasing and tactful interpersonal skills. From the beginning she has manifested a clear professional credibility: 'Mrs King gave you the impression she had lots of experience in the classroom and dealing with special needs' (*Mrs Fox*). She has been able to convince the staff that she knows the stresses and practical problems a teacher meets in the classroom: 'If you get somebody who is like Mrs King who is practical, down-to-earth and who has teaching experience then I think the credibility is quite safe' (*Miss Cooper*). Mr Green confirmed this impression of practical good sense: 'I think if you had a problem she'd answer you in terms that you understood, rather than at some philosophical level that in some ways would be useless'.

Establishing professional credibility is a major issue for both the CISS personnel and the client school staff. Mrs King has been able to do this in Stancliffe but she has been given the opportunity there in a positive climate rather than in a 'show us what you can do' atmosphere. In a less positive climate she may have found it more difficult to display her skills, though being able to respond in a negative stressful atmosphere would seem to be a necessary pre-requisite for a CISS support teacher. Certainly a comment from Mr Green betrayed an underlying feeling that Mrs King is an expert coming from without: 'I personally see her as the expert because she knows a lot more than I do'. The danger of this perception is that it may undermine the concept of support being the sharing of enabling skills in an attempt to meet special needs. Mrs Fox certainly felt that she worked very much as an equal with Mrs King and that together they produced a worthwhile outcome: 'Once we got into this record-keeping, it was very sort of bouncing off each other ideas ... we were actually doing something and at the end of it ... it was quite a sense of achievement that this had been done'.

By her actions Mrs King has given not only herself, but also CISS as a whole, a great deal of credibility in the school. This would make it easier for anyone else from CISS to come and work in the school. 'I think she would be accepted anywhere in the school. What I do think is that she also builds up a certain amount of confidence in someone else working with them. (*Miss Cooper*). Stancliffe appears to have been a school in which a CISS support teacher has met a positive climate and been able to respond with interpersonal and professional skills to create a very successful initial interrelationship. The very personal aspect came through very strongly in the interviews and it is this aspect, in particular, that has made CISS very different from previous support systems. 'I think that the one ... link is very helpful ... and reassuring. We know that that person intends to keep in touch with us and we can get in touch when required, and that's something people didn't have before' (*Miss Cooper*).

Some doubts

What has emerged so far in this case study has been a very positive picture of CISS involvement in Stancliffe First School. Despite the problems created by the head's illness and CISS staffing difficulties, a strong relationship has developed between the CISS support teachers and the staff of the school. The interviews with Mrs King, Miss Cooper and Mrs Fox all revealed a strong mutual respect and affection. Mr Green, however, raised a couple of points which were not so positive.

He came to the school after CISS had already been involved for a term. As well as taking over all the other professional duties of a head, he had to begin negotiating a further contract with CISS via Mrs King. His perceptions of CISS had been developed at his previous school, where the input had been received with mixed feelings. He decided, quite understandably, to let Miss Cooper and Mrs Fox carry on dealing with CISS until he had more time and a greater awareness of what exactly CISS's role was in the school. He quickly hit a snag:

> To me it seemed sensible that the two people who knew most about CISS . . . should actually contact CISS to decide what we were going to do next. On reflection that wasn't the right thing to do. It was my responsibility which shouldn't be passed on to someone else. But that caused a bit of an upset because they were ringing CISS rather than me. (*Mr Green*)

This raises the point of protocol within the system. There are arguments both for and against involving the head in every communication. Heads need to know what is going on but at the same time they are very busy and need to delegate. Mr Green was in a difficult position – new to headship, only acting – and he realized afterwards what he should have done. The point to make here is that he was uncertain as to the correct procedure. Fortunately the school had developed a positive relationship with CISS. His situation would have been much more difficult if the relationship had been fraught with antipathy and misunderstanding, though the crisis created by this situation may well have dictated firmer personal action than was needed at Stancliffe.

When a new head arrives in a school, then, it would be beneficial if the CISS coordinator or an assistant coordinator made a visit to clarify the existing situation and practice. Mr Green met three different people, an assistant coordinator, senior support teacher and support teacher, who confused him, mainly because they visited to discuss the future before he was totally aware of what had happened in the past.

It would be in CISS's interests, in public relations terms, to make sure all new heads are completely knowledgeable about CISS's role, and their past involvement in the school needs to be candidly reviewed. A change of head provides a good opportunity for a change of input style if appropriate.

Mr Green also raised another issue which he felt could lead to a more negative appraisal of CISS's input into the school:

I think if we'd have got involved with children then it might be that I did have negative comments. But because we've just been talking...we've been dealing with CISS and we've been talking about record-keeping and INSET, that has gone well...It's my experience from dealing with CISS before that once you start getting to the level where you are talking about children and dealing with children, the whole system seems so slow that the classroom teachers start getting upset. They feel that they are not getting the support from CISS that they deserve. (*Mr Green*)

He felt that there were children in the school who needed CISS's support because of their special needs. If he were the permanent head then there is no doubt that he would ask for help in the next term for these children, despite the staff's apparent willingness to meet their needs unaided. Experience in his previous school had convinced him that dealing with individual children was where CISS really had problems with credibility, particularly in terms of response time.

There is no certainty that he would find the same problem at Stancliffe. The school's existing attitude to special needs may well have removed the critical urgency for action found in another school. Again the point to be made is that Mr Green has a mixed perception of CISS and it is therefore important that this is discussed as part of an early meeting with someone from the CISS executive.

Reflections

On examining the relationship between CISS and Stancliffe First School, the feeling quickly emerges that this is a good example of how two organizations can interact to their mutual advantage. The original contact and negotiations took place in a receptive atmosphere and the subsequent work that was done had a positive effect throughout the school. A bond of respect and affection built up between the participants and a strong feeling of mutual support developed. Mrs King felt that the staff at Stancliffe understood her role. She enjoyed visiting the school because she received a warm welcome, which contrasted her reception in some other schools. The outcome of the first contract was, therefore, a positive beginning despite early staffing problems and changes in both organizations.

The arrival of Mr Green has apparently not caused drastic changes. After an uncertain start with respect to CISS, he has gradually found his feet and the positive relationship has continued. Mrs King is still popularly received in the school and the INSET she is running in the second contracted period started well. The overwhelming impression after interviewing everybody and making visits to the school was that the CISS involvement at Stancliffe had thrived despite certain problems.

This chapter was part-authored by Paul Geldeart.

Chapter 11
Attitudes to Integration and Support

So far this book has considered a variety of aspects of supporting children and young people with special educational needs in mainstream schools. We have investigated the nature of the support that might be provided and other factors associated with the delivery of the support service.

In this chapter we turn away from the support service(s) to those who are central in providing the majority of time and learning support to the children in question, namely mainstream teachers. It is a general characteristic of new LEA support systems, as exemplified by our evaluation of City LEA, that the bulk of support is provided by such teachers. This is, of course, a major change from the time when a smaller proportion of children were considered to have special educational needs, and the vast majority were allocated to special schools or groups.

The new system, however, requires class teachers both to recognize that a proportion of each class has special educational needs, and that the major responsibility for meeting these needs lies with them. Their ability to meet these needs will in part be improved by training, by direct teaching support, both to relieve pressure and to provide models, and by support staff advising and bringing in specific curriculum materials. However, a fundamental factor beyond these is the teachers' attitudes to the children and the task. Do they see this as their job? Do they view themselves as competent?

In this chapter we shall consider the attitudes of teachers and the influence they have on helping children with special educational needs in mainstream settings.

The Origins of Teachers' Attitudes

It is likely that teachers' attitudes to integration will be affected by several factors. These include the following.

1. Concept of special needs

The teacher's concept of special needs will comprise notions of the type of disability, its prevalence and the need likely to be exhibited by the child. Teachers might have a broad view of the population. They might, on the other hand, limit their definition to children with severe or profound impairments.

2. Experience

Teachers vary in their experience of children with special needs both with respect to their length of time teaching and the type of population they have served. A teacher who has spent 20 years in an affluent suburb may have a much more limited experience than a teacher of five years experience in an inner city. Also, teachers vary in their personal experience of disabilities, their own or those of close friends and relatives.

3. Support available

Schools vary greatly in the arrangements they make for children with special needs. Some offer extra help from within their own resources. This provision, the traditional remedial teacher, is in decline as schools are forced to cut back. Similarly local education authorities (LEAs) vary in the provision they make to schools either directly through staffing and capitation, or through support services (such as special needs support teachers, educational psychologists).

4. Personal ideology

Teachers vary in their view of what they want to contribute and derive from teaching. For some it is a matter of stimulating learning. Others are more concerned with education as the development of interpersonal and social skills. Thus, some focus on the subject matter, while others want to develop the whole child. The presence of children who pose difficulties is a problem from a practical point of view for all teachers. For the teacher more concerned with subject matter, such pupils are an even greater concern.

5. Societal norms

Schools are part of the wider society. Over the past 10 or 20 years there has been a greater awareness of the needs of people with disabilities. Although there is a long way to go, there have been some changes. Long-stay, segregated and secluded hospitals have been closed. Better facilities for physically disabled people have been incorporated into buildings. The general public is now more likely to encounter people or aspects of the environment (signs, ramps and so on) which bring the issues of disability and special needs into their consciousness.

6. Interactions

Attitudes are frequently the result of interactions. Thus positive attitudes to integration may in turn be related to differences not simply in one factor (such as personal ideology) but to interactions of two or more factors. For example, those with a particular child-centred ideology may not be in favour of integration; this opinion may vary in relation to their experience of, for example, levels of support. The study by Thomas (1985) discussed below, and our own study, show this clearly.

The nature of the child's problem

Several studies have revealed that teachers have different views on integration depending upon the type of child under consideration.

Bowman (1989) reports a study of teachers in 14 countries: Egypt, Jordan, Columbia, Mexico, Venezuela, Botswana, Senegal, Zambia, Australia, Thailand, Czechoslovakia, Italy, Norway and Portugal. These varied in terms of the development of their educational systems in general and of special education in particular. In some, integration was a statutory requirement while in others it was being done informally. A sample of 100 teachers was taken from each country, with a final total of nearly 1000.

The teachers were found to favour different types of child for integration into ordinary classes. The summary of these findings is presented in Table 11.1. It can be seen that for each type of condition there is a substantial range of perceived suitability for integration across the countries. The smallest range was 33 per cent, for moderate mental handicap, while the largest was 68 per cent, for the deaf. Thus for the latter, while in at least one country *no* teacher considered deaf children should be integrated, in at least one other over two-thirds were in favour of integration.

Table 11.1: Percentage of teachers favouring integration into ordinary classes

Nature of problem	Median (%)	Range among countries (%)	Size of range (%)
Delicate	75.5	39–97	58
Physical handicap	63.0	28–93	65
Specific learning difficulty	54.0	27–92	65
Speech defect	50.0	26–88	62
Severe emotional and behavioural difficulties	38.0	17–63	46
Moderate mental handicap	31.0	17–50	33
Blind	23.5	0–67	67
Deaf	22.5	0–68	68
Multiple handicaps	7.5	1–54	53
Severe mental handicap	2.5	1–47	46

Source: Bowman (1989).

Despite this variability it can be seen that there is a general hierarchy of conditions that are more or less regarded as possible for integration. Severe mental handicap and multiple handicaps were all considered least favourably, while medical and physical conditions were seen as most easy to manage. Overall, about a quarter of teachers felt that children with sensory impairments could be taught in mainstream classrooms, while less than 10 per cent held this view for children with severe intellectual impairment and multiple handicaps.

Interestingly, Bowman reports that the country where teachers returned high percentages in favour of integration has a law requiring integration. On the other hand, the country with the most sophisticated segregated special education system returned low percentages in favour (0 to 28 per cent), except for delicate children.

Another large-scale study was conducted by Ward and Center (1987) in New South Wales, Australia. The attitudes of 548 school principals, 2219 regular teachers and 332 resource/special education teachers all in current employment in primary schools were investigated by means of a questionnaire. Unlike the Bowman study, Ward and Center also listed disability conditions expressed in educational and behavioural terms in addition to categories of disability. Items included:

- short attention span;
- enuretic child;
- needs typewriter;
- aggressive child;

in addition to

- has profound hearing loss;
- blind;
- multi-handicapped.

Teachers were asked to rate on a scale from one to five their willingness to include in a regular classroom children who displayed the characteristics listed in the 30-item table. Importantly, they were asked to make these judgements given the amount of resources currently available.

The study produced several interesting findings. Firstly there was great similarity between the three groups. Secondly, there was support for the view that teachers are concerned about the more particular behaviours of children, rather than their category of disability, when making judgements on suitability for integration. Thirdly, the authors suggested that the teachers were grouping the various characteristics with regard to the demands made on them in terms of additional time, assistance or skills required.

Finally we will mention a study by Thomas (1985). This investigated the attitudes of 550 teachers, 267 from Tucson, Arizona, USA, and 283 from Devon, UK, to the integration of the 'intellectually handicapped' – those with moderate learning difficulties. Within each geographical sample there were approximately equal numbers drawn from primary and secondary teachers, principals, special class teachers and other special educators. The method adopted by Thomas allowed him to investigate the interaction of personality variables (conservatism, for example) with support factors for each of these groups of teachers.

Thomas found that the best single predictor of attitude to integration was that which the contact special educator appeared to have (such as a visiting advisory teacher or a special class teacher). That is, if this attitude was perceived as positive, the class teacher's attitude was more likely to be positive. This is, perhaps, unexceptional, but Thomas also suggests that where the contact special educator had a neutral or unknown attitude, it had a similar effect to a negative attitude.

However, the interaction with a measure of teachers' confidence was interesting. For those teachers whose contact special educator was seen as having a positive attitude to integration it was confidence in selecting appropriate teaching methods and materials that influenced their responses. Those who saw themselves as competent tended to be more positive towards integration. Thus, although confidence in selecting teaching methods was not in itself an important factor for the whole sample, it becomes significant when seen in relation to the perceived attitudes of contact special educators.

Thomas's study also suggests that there is not a simple inverse relationship between attitudes to integration and the amount of daily responsibility for children in an integrated setting. There was a general tendency for such a relationship to exist, but withdrawal teachers in the Devon sample were more positive overall than their heads, and no different in their degree of support from Devon's peripatetic remedial teachers.

The types of support available

The study by Bowman (1989) also investigated teachers' views in the 14 countries surveyed on the types of help they favoured. Table 11.2 shows the percentages of teachers who considered each type of assistance to be important. The teachers were not forced to choose between each type, nor to rate its importance, so the findings tend to show a general welcome for all the types of help suggested – not a very surprising result, perhaps. However, the variability between countries is again evident, although this is less so than in the views on integration.

It is also interesting to note that smaller classes are rated as important by large numbers of teachers (median 93 per cent); additional help in the classroom is less welcomed (74 per cent). These

Table 11.2: Forms of help rated important by teachers

Form of help	Median (%)	Range among countries (%)	Size of range (%)
Training in individual teaching methods	93	88–100	12
Smaller classes	93	59–100	41
Help and advice for parents	90	72–96	24
Special equipment	89	83–98	15
Support from education advisers	88	72–93	21
Freedom to change curriculum and methods	83	73–93	20
Support from medical staff	81	75–98	23
Training in classroom organization	80	57–94	37
Training in the use of special equipment	79	64–95	31
Parental help with school work at home	78	66–87	21
Additional help in the classroom	74	49–96	47
Support from social services	70	41–79	38

Source: Bowman (1989).

teachers also favoured being trained in developing individual teaching programmes. Bowman also reports that support from education advisers was sought, including psychologists, special teachers and educational welfare officers.

A study in England by Gipps *et al.* (1987) investigated the attitudes of 254 teachers in six LEAs to five different types of support. Unlike the Bowman study, these teachers had to rank the five options and so could not simply ask for 'more of everything'.

These teachers showed an interesting similarity with those in the Bowman study. They also put smaller classes at the top and assistance in the classroom towards the bottom. Moreover, the English sample put advice/in-service training at the bottom of their list. These two studies will be considered further in relation to our own study in one LEA (see also Chapter 6).

Historical changes

In her review of research in the USA on attitudes to integration, Wood (1989) suggests that there has been a general change from negative to positive. Studies in the 1970s tended to reveal sceptical attitudes. Both school principals and classroom teachers were concerned that integration would be problematic – it would be time-consuming; teachers lacked expertise; support was not available.

However, more recent studies have suggested that teachers' attitudes have become more positive. This change has progressed more quickly among primary than secondary teachers, although concerns still exist. What seems to have occurred is that teachers have discovered that although there are problems and challenges, the children are not a completely different group requiring entirely different approaches. As they have worked with the children they have become more realistic in their attitudes and approaches. They still recognize the need for extra training, assistance or provision in some cases, but they also see how the children are essentially part of the whole group.

However, while the general development is in a positive direction, it is important also to examine the possible variation between different professionals, and indeed the parents and children themselves. Szaday *et al.* (1989), for example, argue that those with the most positive attitudes to integration might be those with the least direct contact. For example, a study by Horne (1983) found that teachers believed those most in favour of integration were outsiders – college professors, educational researchers, school psychologists. These teachers considered that those least in favour were pupils without special needs, their parents and regular classroom teachers.

This clearly is a danger – the well-known phenomenon of the enthusiasm of the uninvolved versus the reluctance of the front-line worker. On the other hand, there are some small-scale studies which support a wider positive view of integration by those in the front line – teachers and parents. Hellier (1988), for example, reports a study of six primary schools in the Tayside region of Scotland where children with severe learning difficulties were being integrated. Nineteen educators responded to a questionnaire. The results produced: 'an exceptionally positive reply from the vast majority of educators who have had direct experience of integrating' (p. 78). Not only did these teachers favour integration for the children with special needs, they also mentioned positive effects on their own development.

A study of parent opinion to the integration of children in three integrated primary resources in Sheffield is described by Lindsay (1989). In this study the parents, mainly mothers, showed a very high level of satisfaction with the integrated resource. This mirrored an earlier study (Lindsay and Desforges, 1986) of the views of parents of children in integrated nurseries.

The City Study

In our study we surveyed teachers and heads to investigate their attitude towards special needs and the types of support appropriate for children with special educational needs. We were able to sample teachers from both the part of the LEA which had the new system of support (CISS) and from that area which still had the previous system.

The investigation made use of two main approaches: a large-scale questionnaire survey and interviews with individual heads and special needs coordinators (SENCs). The questionnaire was sent to a total of 654 heads and teachers. Of these, 351 (316 teachers, 35 heads) were in CISS schools and 303 (268 teachers, 35 heads) were in non-CISS schools.

The sample was drawn from nursery, first, middle and upper schools. All CISS nursery and upper school heads were surveyed. In all other cases a *random sample* of respondents was drawn, designed to give approximately equal numbers from CISS and non-CISS schools. (Full details of the sample are presented in Wallwork, 1990.)

The CISS and non-CISS samples were equivalent in terms of length of teaching, grade structure and teacher role (head, special needs coordinator, class teacher, year tutor). The overall response rate was 61.1 per cent with almost identical rates for CISS and non-CISS groups (61.2 and 61.0 per cent, respectively), and similar rates for teachers and heads, and for respondents from different phases.

From this study, therefore, we can examine the views of a large number of teachers, and also compare those in receipt of a new method of support for special educational needs (SEN).

Attitudes to special needs

1. Percentage of children with SEN
Both CISS and non-CISS respondents suggested prevalence rates similar to national estimates – 18.8 per cent overall (19.7 per cent for

CISS and 17.8 per cent for non-CISS respondents, a non-significant difference). Of course, there was variation within each group, with some suggesting 'all children will have special needs at some time'. Some suggested over 90 per cent, but one head estimated 1.6 per cent. A variation is inevitable, and realistic given the different catchment areas of schools. But a difference of this magnitude suggests that the 'high' estimators have a different concept of SEN from that of the DES.

The issue of bilingual children was raised specifically by some, since the 1981 Education Act (GB.DES, 1981) does not cover learning difficulties *specifically* related to English being a second language. This has caused confusion and concern nationally. The lack of bilingual teachers and psychologists has created difficulties in determining the exact nature of a particular child's developmental status. For example, is the child's educational progress limited by a lack of development of English, or by a more generalized learning difficulty?

2. Inappropriate placement of children with SEN

Again, the two groups did not differ statistically in their views. In each case about two-fifths felt that some children were inappropriately placed. However, this resulted from a concern about the perceived lack of resources. Many expressed a desire to support the children in mainstream schools:

> It's the support that's inappropriate not the principle of mainstreaming.

> If the support provided is efficient then all special education needs children should be in mainstream.

> Mainstream provision must expand and cater for a wider range of individual needs.

Of course, not all respondents felt like this. Some considered that there were children whose needs were such that, in their opinion, a mainstream placement was not appropriate. some expressed concern for the progress of others: 'Some children bring down the general standard in classes where they are present'.

Thus, throughout the authority there were teachers concerned about integration – as they see it. This concern appears mainly to be driven by an anxiety that resources are not sufficient to make integration work. The results were not significantly different in CISS and non-CISS schools.

3. Most difficult type of special need

Respondents varied in their views regarding the most difficult special need to meet. However, the two main categories were learning difficulties and, to a greater extent, emotional and behavioural difficulties. Indeed, as can be seen from Table 11.3, these two categories together were chosen by almost all the respondents.

Table 11.3: Most difficult special need to meet

Special need	CISS respondents (%)	Non-CISS respondents (%)
Learning difficulties	34	35
Emotional and behavioural	60	58
Visual impairment	1.4	0.6
Hearing impairment	1.4	1.7
Physical impairment	0.9	3.3
Other	2.4	2.8

Interviews with the heads reinforced the particular concerns felt in meeting the special needs of, and problems posed by, children with emotional and behavioural difficulties. The very small numbers choosing sensory and physical impairments probably reflects the relative infrequency of such children and the more pressing needs of the two groups most prevalent. Again, there are no statistically significant differences between CISS and non-CISS respondents.

These findings are not in line with those reported by Bowman (1989; see Table 11.1). City LEA teachers were more likely to doubt their ability to meet the special needs of children with emotional and behavioural problems; in Bowman's study this was half way down the list. On the other hand, sensory impairments were seen as relatively less problematic than by Bowman's respondents.

4. Pupil–teacher ratio (PTR)

The sample was asked whether the PTR had changed over the previous 18 months. About half of each group considered it had remained the same and 32 per cent of CISS and 25 per cent of non-CISS respondents believed it had worsened.

However, once more there was no statistically significant difference between the two groups.

5. Do the CISS and non-CISS samples differ?

These findings are important in judging whether the two groups differ on important dimensions. In fact, on all the measures described above the two groups are very similar, and there are no statistically significant differences in these results. The two groups have similar teaching experience generally, and they hold similar views on integration and meeting children's special educational needs.

We can now look at the groups' views on the services they have received, reasonably confident in the view that any differences found are likely to be the result of the impact of those services rather than extraneous factors.

How should special needs be met?

We asked our sample to rate five ways of helping children with special needs, namely:

- withdrawal to regular sessions;
- individual teaching programmes/materials;
- assistance in the classroom;
- advice/in-service training for class teachers;
- smaller classes so the class teacher can cope.

We were able to compare the results for:

- City LEA versus a national sample (the study of six LEAs by Gipps *et al.*, 1987) and Bowman's (1989) international study;
- CISS versus non-CISS teachers;
- those who had attended a special needs course versus those who had not;
- those who had attended a skills delivery course versus those who had not. This was a course aimed at giving teachers practical skills to help them work with children with SEN in their classroom.

All three samples gave a high priority to smaller classes. The Gipps sample placed this as top priority (out of five) while Bowman's respondents and our sample placed it second (from a range of 12 and 5 options, respectively). However, our sample placed assistance in the classroom as top priority. This was placed fourth out of five in the Gipps study and 11th of 12 by Bowman's sample.

Withdrawal of children to regular sessions outside the classroom was not an option in the Bowman study. This was popular among Gipps's respondents (second out of five), but our two subsamples differed in their opinions of this option. A significantly greater number of CISS respondents gave this a high ranking, compared with non-CISS colleagues. (Thirty-three per cent of CISS respondents placed it first or second, compared with 19 per cent of non-CISS.)

This is, perhaps, a surprising result. Why should teachers in the schools covered by CISS want *more* withdrawal? Does this imply a criticism of the CISS approach, and their use of INSET and advice? An answer to these questions can be found when we examine the effects of attendance on relevant courses on SEN. Here we find an interesting interaction. Course attendees in CISS schools were more likely to place withdrawal low and INSET/advice high in their preference list.

Thus, it appears that it is not CISS or attendance at such courses *alone* but the *two together* that is important. Teachers and heads in CISS schools who have attended the Authority's courses on special needs are more favourable towards the benefits of INSET and advice, and less in favour of withdrawal, as a means of providing support for SEN children. This finding applied to special needs courses in general, and no similar result was found for attendance on skills delivery courses in particular.

Feelings towards the help received

The sample was asked to state their opinion of the adequacy of the help received for special needs. Again, we can compare CISS and non-CISS groups, and City LEA against a national sample. Table 11.4 shows the results for the two CISS groups, and a national sample (see Gipps *et al.*, 1987). This distribution was also common across first and upper, but not middle schools.

Table 11.4: Feelings towards the help received for special needs

Perception of help received	CISS respondents (%)	Non-CISS respondents (%)	National respondents (%)
Good	1	2	3
Adequate	21	15	33
Inadequate	52	65	54
Totally inadequate	25	17	10

It would appear that the City LEA sample overall (combining CISS and non-CISS respondents) was more negative about the support they had received than the national comparison sample.

When we look more closely at the two City LEA groups we find an interesting result – two conflicting trends. It appears that the CISS sample has become more polarized, in both directions. There are more CISS respondents who are reasonably satisfied and describe the support as 'adequate' (21 versus 15 per cent) *but* also more who are very dissatisfied and describe it as 'totally inadequate' (25 versus 17 per cent). This was the case for respondents be they deputy heads, class teachers or year tutors, but heads of CISS schools were the most positive with 33 per cent considering the service adequate or better. Why is this? Table 11.5 suggests some answers.

Table 11.5: Relationship between CISS respondents' views of the support they had received and the change in proportion of children with SEN

Proportion of SEN children	Good (%)	Adequate (%)	Inadequate (%)	Totally inadequate (%)
Increased/stayed the same	1	12	48	38
Decreased	0	31	53	16

Further analysis suggested that it was *not* related to respondents' estimates of the percentage of children with SEN, but was related to perceived *changes* in the proportion of children with SEN over the previous 18 months. CISS respondents who considered that the proportion had increased were more likely to consider support inadequate (38 versus 16 per cent). The trend was similar, but less marked among non-CISS respondents (26 versus 9 per cent, respectively).

Similarly CISS respondents who considered that the proportion had stayed the same were more satisfied than those who felt it had increased (31 versus 12 per cent choosing 'adequate').

Length of teaching experience was also a relevant factor. In CISS schools, for example, the less experienced teachers were more positive and the most experienced were more critical; but these attitudes are also influenced by the perceived demands caused by an increased number of SEN children, in CISS schools particularly.

Thus CISS respondents in general appear more polarized in their views on the quality of the support they have been receiving.

Teacher Attitudes – An Overview

In this chapter we have considered some findings from our study of one LEA on teacher attitudes to special needs and support for SEN children, and compared these results with other studies in England and internationally.

It is apparent that there is no simple picture in terms of teacher attitudes. There is some evidence that attitudes have shifted in favour of integrating children with SEN over the past ten years or so. This is partly the result of the experiences teachers have had: they have developed some competence; they have not been 'swamped' as some feared at the time of publication of the Warnock Report (GB.DES, 1978). Also, our study suggests that younger teachers may be more positive in their attitudes to integration.

Teachers from the different studies have varied in their views on which children they consider could be supported in mainstream, or have the most difficult needs to meet. There are some major differences across groups of teachers in different countries. We suggest this variation will reflect the levels and the history of support in each setting – there are likely to be variations across LEAs in the UK. For example, the integration of hearing impaired children is highly advanced in the UK; in some LEAs all children will be in a form of integrated setting. Support systems in the form of units, peripatetic teachers and so on are often well developed. Compare this with the large number of schools for children with learning difficulties, for example, which still exist.

Teachers' attitudes to support have also been examined more analytically in our study. Our results suggest that these attitudes can be affected by several interacting factors. Thus, the teachers in CISS schools, where support had a greater emphasis on advice and INSET and relatively less on direct teaching of children than in non-CISS schools, were polarized and were more likely to consider this form of support to be better *and* worse than that received before. This polarization was related to the perceived change in the number of SEN children – those teachers who thought there were more SEN children were less positive about the new system and vice versa.

We do not know whether the *actual* number of SEN children in these teachers' schools had changed and so directly influenced their opinions, or whether it was entirely a *perceived* change. Whichever, it is apparent that the teachers' attitudes were affected by how they related the support that was available to the demands they felt were being made of them.

We have also shown that attendance on courses can interact with the type of support received and so affect attitudes. Teachers whose support had changed to comprise a higher level of advice and provision of INSET and a reduction of direct support for individual children differed in their opinions of this new system. Those who had attended SEN courses were more positive than those who had not, and they also considered this type of provision to be better than that they used to receive.

Thus our study supports that of Thomas (1985) in finding that interactions between factors are important in determining attitudes to integration. A general conclusion might be that while teachers have come to accept and even encourage the integration of children with special needs, these positive attitudes must be fostered by adequate support and training.

This chapter draws substantially on a study by Andrew Wallwork.

Chapter 12
Looking Forward to Supportive Education in the 1990s

In this book we have concentrated on support service delivery for children with special educational needs in mainstream schools. We have drawn particularly upon the research we carried out in one large local educational authority during 1987 to 1989, and have related this to other work by ourselves and others. In this chapter we now wish to sketch some more general considerations for the future development of supportive education: what changes can we anticipate in schools' and LEAs' provision for learners with SEN?

Answering this question is of course very difficult at this time because of the present socio-political situation. In this context, special needs issues tend to come a long way down the line of consideration. Consequently, in this final chapter we shall consider the implications for the way forward based both on an educational research basis (for example the work presented in this book) and on an ideological commitment to integrative educational systems.

Integration

There can be little doubt now that the basic educational system for all children with special educational needs should be one which is integrated with the mainstream. This is primarily a question of rights. As Newell (1985) has argued:

We see ending segregation not first as a complex educational and professional issue, weighing up the advantages and disadvantages of two settings for meeting special needs, but first as a social and political issue, pursuing the human right not to be segregated outside the mainstream. (p. 23)

The Fish Report (ILEA, 1985) followed a consideration by the Inner London Education Authority of its provision for children with special educational needs, and this came out in favour of a system based upon integration. More recently other LEAs have also been reviewing their provision and have produced either policy statements or discussion documents which also further this approach. Certainly this is the view taken by the special education review team that considered the systems in Sheffield LEA, an authority famed for its extensive provision for children with special educational needs, but with a history of large numbers of special schools (Lindsay *et al.*, 1990).

In our view, it is important to go beyond the rhetoric of 'rights'. What is more important is what actually happens to the child. We agree with the statement by Hegarty, Pocklington and Lucas (1981): 'Pupils with special educational needs do not need integration: they need education'. This is not to deny the rights issue, but to build upon it. As Lindsay (1985) has argued elsewhere:

The issue now is not *whether* to integrate children but *how* to integrate them, to their advantage, both in the medium term, with respect to their schooling, and in the long-term preparation for life. (p. 7)

The importance of evaluation of successful, and therefore also of unsuccessful, schemes of integration has also been stressed by Danby and Cullen (1988) in their recent review of studies evaluating the effectiveness of integration of mentally handicapped pupils, as they call them. It is their conclusion that: 'the research to date has not begun to form the basis of such an evaluation' (p. 192).

Finally, we note that the House of Commons, Education, Science and Arts Select Committee (1987), which investigated the implementation of the 1981 Education Act, also stressed the need for more evaluation. They argued that support for the principle of integration did not necessarily mean that all children should be educated in mainstream rather than special schools:

...integration can and should take place whatever placement is adopted and whatever forms of special educational provision are made. Although it is easier to plan and carry out shared activities when children are in the same school there is no reason for not arranging such activities through collaboration between special schools and other schools. (para. 1)

Given the range of practices with respect to integration that the Committee found across the country, they felt concern at the lack of central guidance:

The Committee concludes that progress towards integrated forms of provision should now be evaluated both in terms of the quality of the educational provision and in terms of the wider appropriateness of the provision, so that greater guidance can be given to LEAs. (para. 20)

We concur with these views. Although we support integrated provision in principle, the fundamental issue is that integration must be seen as a means to equality of opportunity, not as an end in itself. It is also important to recognize the relatively limited amount of research evidence on the subject. The study of City LEA's initiative presented in this book is one additional element in a gradually developing picture of the strengths and weaknesses of various forms of integration.

What we have demonstrated here is the well-known truth that integration is a complex issue. It is not simply removing children from, or never sending them to, segregated special schools. Integration can include supporting children within their local school. But it can also include supporting teachers, and developing their skills, in order that the question of children leaving their mainstream school may not arise (see Hegarty and Moses, 1988).

In institutional terms, integration can include full participation in all class activities through to a child based in a special school attending a mainstream school for specific purposes. The following illustrative examples are drawn from our experience of the continuum of integration in another LEA.

School A

This is a mainstream middle school (for children in years 4 to 7, age 8 to 12 years). Physically, it has a traditional box classroom design. In addition to its local intake, there is a designated integrated resource.

There are 2.5 full-time equivalent teachers plus some extra money for capitation, allocated by the LEA to support 24 children on statements of special educational needs.

This school decided to organize its staffing so that 1.5 teachers were added to the resource teachers, making four in all. All the children on statements (five per year group) were placed full-time in mainstream classes. These classes were each given an extra teacher. The class sizes are relatively large, about 30 plus, but the two teachers are able to work 'in tandem', to use the school's terminology.

At the present time, this system has been in operation for over four years and appears popular with children, parents and staff. An evaluation of the system by one of us (Geoff Lindsay) and a trainee educational psychologist is currently underway.

School B

This school is a partly open-plan junior and infant school (reception to year 6, age 5 to 11 years). There is also a nursery.

The nursery is one of three in mainstream schools across the city which have been designated special integrated nurseries. In addition to local intake, up to 12 children with special educational needs are admitted. For this group there are one teacher and one nursery nurse. These children have a range of difficulties and needs, but in general have a mild to moderate developmental delay, and speech and language difficulties. A speech therapist visits one day a week.

The primary department has one extra teacher and one child care assistant to support ten children with special educational needs. Many of these will have moved up from the nursery, but others join the school at five years of age. In general, these children are able to follow a mainstream curriculum with support, but one or two have more problematic learning difficulties.

This school organizes itself such that the children are all integrated into classes, and the teachers and non-teaching assistants support them in class for part of the week. Being open-plan, there is no obvious 'withdrawal', but small groups of children, including those on statements, can be formed as part of the normal routine.

School C

This is a junior school for children in years 3 to 6 (age 7 to 11 years). Up to 20 children are also admitted on statements. These children have mild or specific learning difficulties. In practice they tend to be youngsters who have significant problems with literacy, despite otherwise adequate abilities, which have proven very resistant to improvement through the help normally available in primary schools in the city.

Children attend this school normally for between one and two years full-time, after which they return to their original mainstream schools. While attending School C, they spend much of their time in one of two classes, each of which has a teacher for up to ten children and a non-teaching assistant shared between the two classes. While in these classes they receive intensive small group and individual work, they also join in other activities with children in the main body of the school.

School D

This is a secondary school for young people with moderate learning difficulties. It currently has 82 pupils from years 8 to 11 (age 12 to 16 years). It is the only special school in the authority for secondary pupils with these problems; there are also three integrated resources in mainstream secondary schools.

Pupils in this school normally transfer from the authority's one primary special school for children with moderate learning difficulties. Some, however, move from integrated resources at the age of transfer, or perhaps during their secondary school careers.

This school is developing links with integrated resources in mainstream schools. Some pupils from the school visit a resource on a part-time basis for specific activities. If this develops a more extended placement, even full-time transfer, is possible.

On the other hand some learners in the resource visit the special school, also on a part-time basis.

School D operates a similar system with the authority's school for secondary age young people with severe learning difficulties. Again, there is a two-way interchange of pupils for specific purposes, either individuals or groups.

These four brief descriptions indicate only part of one authority's range of provision for pupils with special educational needs. However, even here the variety is evident. Further examples can be found in Baker and Bovair (1989), Dessent (1987) and in Appendix 2 of the Fish Report (ILEA, 1985).

To return to our earlier point, integration is not a simple unitary concept. Increasingly teachers and authorities are developing systems of schooling which incorporate children with special educational needs within the general body of provision. Indeed, recent information from the DES suggests that about one-third of all pupils with statements are now educated within mainstream schools. The figures for January 1989 for schools in England are given in Table 12.1.

Table 12.1: Numbers of pupils with statements of SEN in January 1989 for schools in England

Type of school	Children with statements	Proportion of the school population (%)
All schools	155,191	2.1
Special schools	102,064	1.4
Mainstream schools	53,127	0.7

There has been a substantial development of integration, in terms of where children are educated, over the past decade. However, we would argue that this simple measure of integration is not enough – we need to know how effective the provision is. We shall return to the question of evaluation later.

The Effects of the 1988 Education Reform Act

The 1988 Education Reform Act (ERA) (GB.DES, 1988a) is the most comprehensive legislation to be directed at education since the 1944 Education Act (GB.ME, 1944) which laid down the direction for the next 40 or more years. At the current time (mid-1990) the education system is reeling from the impact of the legislation. Teacher morale is very low and a large number of chief education officers have retired or resigned over the past few years.

Interestingly, and indeed depressingly, special educational needs are in no way a major concern of this legislation. Having followed the conception, gestation, birth and now faltering footsteps of this infant, we have the impression that wherever special educational needs have been considered this has been as an afterthought, or as a marginal issue. Major and sustained pressure from the professionals, parents and voluntary bodies has gradually changed the initial proposals. Some of these developments have been intrinsically sound, but others have been attempts at damage limitation.

One fundamental difficulty with the ERA was its genesis, from different and in some ways opposing and conflicting ideologies. This has been examined acutely by Lawton (1988, 1989). Of particular concern are the efforts of those who sought a 'free market' approach to education, compared with those who sought to develop a system which ensured minimum standards. In simple terms, the development of Local Management of Schools (LMS) is an example of the former, while the National Curriculum and its accompanying assessment programme is an example of the latter.

This uneasy alliance of competing ideologies has itself produced many problems, with significant power shifts away from LEAs towards both the centre (the DES) and the schools. Governing bodies are now more powerful, but only within the constraints set by government and, to a decreasing degree, by the LEA. At a time of significant cutbacks, governors are challenging this 'power', which in many cases has become the ability to cut teaching posts in order to meet the demands of a budget which must be based on a formula limited by legislation. These problems have become even more fraught in those LEAs where charge-capping has led to further large reductions in the LEA budget, which must lead to further job losses, particularly among teachers.

Where does this leave special educational needs? We present here some of the major difficulties in this area.

National Curriculum

What should be the curriculum of pupils with SEN? Should it include all the National Curriculum or only some of it? Is it meaningful to consider the National Curriculum as relevant to a profoundly handicapped youngster, for example?

The position generally being taken is that if the National Curriculum is a 'good thing' it should be good for all. Consequently the emphasis is placed on *curriculum entitlement*. This is expressed clearly in the National Curriculum Council's (1989) publication *A Curriculum for All*:

> All pupils share the right to a broad and balanced curriculum, including the National Curriculum. The right extends to every

registered pupil of compulsory school age attending a maintained
or grant maintained school, whether or not he or she has a
statement of special educational needs. This right is implied in the
1988 Education Reform Act. (para. 1)

Educationists have generally welcomed this statement, and have
sought to build upon and extend its sentiments. Interesting work is
being carried out in many authorities in developing the curriculum for
pupils, even with the most severe and complex special needs, but
within this normalizing framework.

At this time, therefore, early concerns about the restrictions of the
National Curriculum appear to be lessening. Indeed the then Prime
Minister, in an interview with the *Sunday Telegraph* on 15th April
1990 stated: 'when we first started on this [the National Curriculum] I
do not think I ever thought they would do the syllabus in such detail as
they are doing now'.

Similarly in the area of general education, the advice coming from
the different subject groups developing attainment targets and
programmes of study appears to be more educationally sound and
slightly more flexible than was once feared.

Assessment
The National Curriculum is to be accompanied by a major programme
of assessment. At this time, three consortia are developing
Standard Assessment Tasks (SATs) which were piloted in the early
summer term of 1990. The initial feedback on these trials was a matter
of concern, with heads complaining about the time taken, the strain
on teachers and children, and the questionable reliability of the
exercise.

The Secretary of State has recognized that the extent of assessment
initially envisaged will be impractical and in a press release on 9th
April 1990 stated that he would not impose a statutory requirement to
administer SATs in technology, history or geography at the end of
stage 1 (seven-year-olds).

Thus, there are signs that the extent of assessment will be reduced
both in breadth and degree. But the fundamental concerns about the
whole assessment process have not been fully addressed and the
underlying model in the report of the Task Group on Assessment and
Testing (GB.DES, 1988b), and criticized by Nuttall (1988), still
appears to be that which is being followed.

These general concerns about the scheme as they relate to all children are supplemented by additional worries about the problems faced by children with various forms of learning difficulty or disability. Again, useful guidance has been offered in *A Curriculum for All* (National Curriculum Council, 1989) but it is clear that the system as previously envisaged will pose major problems to pupils with SEN, raising doubts about both the validity of the exercise and the damaging effect on these youngsters' self-esteem. For example what will it be like to be a 'Level 1 child', the kind of label which unfortunately might begin to appear.

Formula funding

LEAs in recent years have, to varying degrees, adopted policies of positive action, directing extra resources to schools with higher numbers of pupils suffering social disadvantage and/or with SEN. Their ability to do this has now been curtailed by the terms of a formula by which schools must be funded in the future. Under this formula, 75 per cent of the money going to schools must be based upon pupil numbers. The remaining 25 per cent provides the opportunity for the LEA to take account of a whole variety of factors which affect real costs – heating, grounds maintenance and cleaning, as well as SEN. As Lindsay (1989) has predicted, one effect of the introduction of this legislation has been to increase the number of referrals for Section 5 assessments, in the hope that some pupils will receive statements, and consequently bring more resources to the school.

This effect has become a reality. For example, in Sheffield the number of referrals for formal assessment of pupils of primary age increased by 61 per cent between 1987 and 1989, from 127 to 205 per annum (Lindsay *et al.*, 1990).

There are other problems with funding for those learners in schools who are not the subject of statements. Although LEAs, in devising the budgets of schools, may build in a factor for SEN, it is within the power of the school to use this money however they wish. Already we have seen examples of this, compounded by budget cuts in absolute terms in some schools. For example, we know of one secondary school in an inner city area that is in danger of losing four of its six staff who work with pupils with SEN. This is the result of the general budget cut leading to a need to lose staff, and the school's internal decision about which staff to shed.

The concern is that, once more, some learners with SEN will be the ones to lose out as these very real cuts take effect.

LMS and special schools
At this time special schools are outside LMS schemes. However, the government has the power to bring them into it and indeed has announced a feasibility study on this.

In one sense their exclusion is an anomaly – if LMS is such a good thing every school should benefit. The reality of the effects on mainstream schools, however, raises considerable alarm. In addition, the impact of strict formula funding on the same basis as at present could be very serious and certainly could inhibit the kinds of flexible arrangements discussed above, whereby pupils have shared access to different facilities. Already some mainstream schools are withdrawing from such arrangements, making their viability very doubtful unless ways are found to build such arrangements into the funding model for special schools.

Integrating Support

How can we organize provision for these learners with special needs that meets our educational objectives, but is also practical under the present legislation? Are ways forward discernible at this time?

Special educational needs

First we need to return to the point made in different ways in various places in this book. Underlying this discussion is a conception of 'special educational needs' and 'learning difficulties'. As we outlined in Chapter 1, these terms are not without problems of definition. Ultimately, these terms are largely the results of the constructs of others, rather than of the children themselves. The problems a child has in developing through the education system are, to varying degrees, the result of factors outside that child. This is not to deny the major disabling effect of certain impairments, but to put these in context. We have experienced many teachers and parents who consider certain provision which they used to think suitable for a child to be so no longer. This is not because the child has changed, but because the provision has. Thus a 'mainstream school placement' may have changed, meaning that detail-class sizes may be larger, other support may have been reduced and teachers may feel less able to work effectively with the child.

Thus it is important to take care in using terms like special educational needs. Indeed it could be argued that the term itself, while generally welcomed when used in the Warnock Report (DES, 1978), has outlived whatever usefulness it might have had: given the problem of definition and the adverse effects such labels can engender, perhaps we should avoid their use.

This critique has much to commend it. We share the concern that the concept of special educational needs might be as divisive, and ultimately as negative, as the concept it replaced. However, inevitably the term is now so much part of educational jargon and indeed legislation that in our view the current strategy should be to explore critically its basis and refine its use rather than argue for its rejection.

Support
In this book we have explored the concept and practice of support. Traditionally this has been represented by visiting professionals, or 'special' staff, working mainly with individual pupils either in mainstream or special schools. Such practice has been subjected to much criticism in recent years.

We have explored a broader view of support and have illuminated this with a study of one particular LEA. Here, support was provided by a team of teachers who also offered several different forms of assistance. These included in-service training, direct teaching of children, collaborative endeavours with teachers in classrooms, joint work in policy-making, and the development of materials and approaches (such as record-keeping).

What is important here is that these types of support are not only different in kind, but are also aimed at different aspects of the system. This system includes the child, but is interactive. Problems are conceptualized as part of an interaction between the child and the wider system (class, school, society). What our study of City Integration Support Service (CISS) revealed was that all of these initiatives have their own validity. However, the notion of balance and the negotiation of such a balance in addition to competence was important for delivery to be seen as acceptable and appropriate.

Teachers, as well as pupils, are now seen as the legitimate clients of such a service. But support must mean more than a generalized sense of well-being. What our study shows is that teachers want to develop real understandings and skills and also to have concrete assistance when necessary. The use of support assistants is one example of how the latter can be implemented. Thus it is not enough merely to be aware, or knowledgeable, or even skilful; a teacher must also have the opportunity to implement such abilities. If this is not available directly from teachers, the use of other workers may be appropriate.

This raises the further issue of the abilities of such support workers. Who is the appropriate person to work in such a role? There is a question mark hanging over the large-scale use of non-qualified adults working with pupils whose educational, and possibly socio-emotional, needs are greater than normal. Do we allocate the most complex operations to the untrained? Would we expect a garage to allocate a major repair to the newest and least experienced recruit?

This is not to deny that amongst this group there are people with excellent bases on which to develop, nor that they have relevant skills. Indeed, many such adults have excellent experience and skills *which they are able to generalize*. But it is this ability to generalize and further to develop their knowledge and skill which are crucial.

Thus, the concept and practice of 'support' have been broadened, but the new practice is not without difficulty. We consider that it is now important to look further towards a system of *integrated support*.

Integrating support
Recent developments in provision for children with special educational needs have, in our view, not always had coherence. They have started from either a position of ideology (such as integration) or *ad hocery* (such as empty buildings becoming available for special schools). While we recognize the importance of the former, and the probable inevitability of the latter, we would urge an approach which considers *children's needs*. In this we go beyond a concept of special educational needs to a broader perspective of the development of all children. In other words, we seek a system of education which is designed to individualize provision to meet the educational and developmental needs of all children.

We do not claim this to be an easy task. Indeed, we recognize that its implementation is made even harder by some aspects of recent legislation, particularly the lack of flexibility apparent in Local

Management of Schools. However, we still consider it important at this time – indeed more so – to reconsider our approach.

We agree with Fish (1989) that it is important to consider a child's requirement through a series of dimensions. We would suggest the following:

1. Curriculum
- the child's curriculum needs, including reference to the National Curriculum;
- the teaching approach, including pace and frequency, and in some cases specialized teaching programmes, materials and support systems (such as signing and bilingual support).

2. Personal and social development
- the support required to develop the whole child, including access to other children who do not have special educational needs taking account of the child's linguistic, ethnic or cultural backgrounds.

3. Teaching environment
- the nature of the classroom, including its size, shape, acoustic and visual properties as appropriate;
- appropriate teaching group including size and the characteristics of the other children.

4. The total school environment
- the size and characteristics of the total school environment(s), including physical resources (such as access), ethos, links with other schools and community.

5. Teaching and non-teaching classroom support
- the resources necessary from teachers, non-teaching assistants, nursery nurses as appropriate.

6. Therapeutic support
- those resources necessary to enable a child to overcome difficulties which are not educational in the narrow sense, but which give rise to special educational needs or other significant personal developmental needs – speech therapy; physiotherapy; counselling and psychotherapy; music, art and drama therapy.

7. *Technical support*
  ● those resources necessary to ensure that the child's access to learning is optimized and maintained by attention to, for example, hearing and vision aids; physical aids and alterations to equipment; making of specific toys and play equipment.

This list is significant in the following ways: firstly, there is nothing specifically 'special'; these factors are applicable to *all* children. Even the categories of therapeutic and teacher support can be applied to so-called normal children. For example, if we adopt a health rather than sickness approach to the development of social competence, happiness and adjustment, we must accept that all children have a need for therapeutic guidance and opportunity. The specific nature of such support may vary, but the basic requirements are identical.

Secondly, what distinguishes children's needs can be found at a more micro level of analysis. This might be the *nature* of the detailed provision (such as one approach to the development of reading rather than another); the *duration* of help or its *intensity*.

Thirdly, there is no simple match between these categories and placement. The concepts of integration and segregation therefore have less direct importance. For example, a particular child may require particular forms of learning to be facilitated in a very intensive small group or one-to-one setting, while others need to be in larger groups. If the former is cognitive in the narrowest sense, and the latter is social, then very different settings may be needed. A child with particular severe learning difficulties may require a distraction-reduced learning environment for developing particular abilities, but the model of other non-impaired children to develop societal competencies.

As stated above, we do not wish to underplay the inherent complexity of what we are suggesting. It is not surprising that previous systems have been understood in an over-simplified way – 'segregated' or 'integrated', for example. However, we believe we can move much further along this line of development, and welcome the examples of some authorities that are examining such approaches (see Lindsay *et al.*, 1990).

Conclusion

In this book we have attempted to present a review of current practice, to relate this to previous endeavours and to suggest the implications of these for the future. Working daily with teachers, we are very aware of the great demands made of them, and the uncertainties which surround them. In the first year of LMS we observed many institutions with a budget insufficient to cover their costs. Teachers are in very short supply in the south-east of England, while in some authorities they are likely to be made redundant. The effects of capping on those authorities considered to have an excessive poll tax have added further confusion and distress.

We are also aware that there are still uncertainties specifically concerning special education and LMS. At this time, the DES is conducting an exercise to judge whether or how to bring special schools into this initiative. While there is much support for the idea of delegating budgets, we hope that the budgets are adequate and that there is flexibility of funding built into this system. A simple head count approach cannot hope to be adequate given the funding some of our most disabled young people require to give anything approaching a suitable education to meet their needs. Also, a system that ties money – all money – to schools too tightly will inhibit if not prevent flexible systems of support from developing.

On the other hand this time may prove to be one of opportunity; certainly these problems have helped to focus the minds of some people. If we can build upon the recent positive developments, and extend them into a new system of integrated, properly resourced support, we shall have had some success.

References

ABRAHAM, J. and LINDSAY, G. (1990). *The Junior Rating Scale.* Windsor: NFER-NELSON.

AINSCOW, M. and MUNCEY, J. (1984). *SNAP.* Cardiff: Drake Educational Associates.

BAKER, D. and BOVAIR, K. (1989). *Making the Special Schools Ordinary?* Volume 1. Lewes: Falmer Press.

BERMAN, P. and McLAUGHLIN, M. (1978). *Federal Programs Supporting Educational Change*, Volume 8, *Implementing and Sustaining Innovations.* California: The Rand Corporation.

BOWMAN, I. (1989). Teacher training and the integration of handicapped pupils: a UNESCO study. In: JONES, N. (Ed.) *Special Educational Needs Review.* London: Falmer Press.

CASHDAN, A. and PUMFREY, P.D. (1969). 'Some effects of the remedial teaching of reading', *Educational Research*, 11, 138–42.

CLAYTON, T. (1989a). 'Making the most of welfare assistants', *Special Children*, May, 8–9.

CLAYTON, T. (1989b). The role of the welfare assistant in supporting children with special educational needs in ordinary primary schools. In: EVANS, R. (Ed.) *Special Educational Needs: Policy and Practice.* Oxford: Blackwell Educational and National Association for Remedial Children.

CLOUGH, P. (1988). 'Bridging the gap between 'mainstream' and 'special' education: a curriculum problem', *Journal of Curriculum Studies.* 20, 4, 327–38.

CLOUGH, P. and LINDSAY, G. (1989). The evaluation of SENISS: the final report. Educational Research Centre Papers, University of Sheffield.

CLOUGH, P. and THOMPSON, D. (1987). Curricular approaches to learning difficulty: problems for the paradigm. In: FRANKLIN, B. (Ed.) *Learning Disabilities: Dissenting Essays.* Lewes: Falmer Press.

COLLINS, J. (1961). The effects of remedial education. Education Monograph, University of Birmingham.

DANBY, J. and CULLEN, C. (1988). 'Integration and mainstreaming: a review of the efficiency of mainstreaming and integration for mentally handicapped pupils', *Educational Psychology*, 8, 177–95.

DESSENT, T. (1983). Who is responsible for children with special needs. In: BOOTH, T. and POTTS, P. (Eds) *Integrating Special Education.* Oxford: Blackwell.

DESSENT, T. (1987). *Making the Ordinary School Special.* Lewes: Falmer Press.

FISH, J. (1989). *What is Special Education?* Milton Keynes: Open University Press.

FROSTIG, M. and HORNE, D. (1964). *The Frostig Programme for the Development of Visual Perception: Teacher's Guide.* Chicago, IL: Follett.

GARNETT, J. (1988). 'Support teaching: taking a closer look', *British Journal for Special Education*, 15, 1.

GIPPS, C., GOLDSTEIN, H. and GROSS, H. (1985). 'Twenty per cent with special educational needs. Another legacy from Cyril Burt?', *Remedial Education*, 20, 2.

GIPPS, C., GROSS, H. and GOLDSTEIN, H. (1987). *Warnock's Eighteen Per Cent: Children with Special Needs in Primary Schools.* London: Falmer Press.

GOLBY, M. and GULLIVER, J. (1979). 'Whose remedies, whose ills? A critical review of remedial education', *Journal of Curriculum Studies*, 11, 137–47.

GREAT BRITAIN. DEPARTMENT OF EDUCATION AND SCIENCE (1975). Circular 2/75: *The Discovery of Children Requiring Special Education and the Assessment of their Needs.* London: HMSO.

GREAT BRITAIN. DEPARTMENT OF EDUCATION AND SCIENCE (1975). The Bullock Report: *A Language for Life.* London: HMSO.

GREAT BRITAIN. DEPARTMENT OF EDUCATION AND SCIENCE (1978). The Warnock Report: *Special Educational Needs.* London: HMSO.

GREAT BRITAIN. DEPARTMENT OF EDUCATION AND SCIENCE (1981). *Education Act 1981.* London: HMSO.

GREAT BRITAIN. DEPARTMENT OF EDUCATION AND SCIENCE (1988a). *Education Reform Act.* London: HMSO.

GREAT BRITAIN. DEPARTMENT OF EDUCATION AND SCIENCE (1988b). *National Curriculum: Task Group on Assessment and Testing.* London: HMSO.

GREAT BRITAIN. DEPARTMENT OF EDUCATION AND SCIENCE (1989a). *Educating Physically Disabled Children: Report by Her Majesty's Inspectorate.* London: HMSO.

GREAT BRITAIN. DEPARTMENT OF EDUCATION AND SCIENCE (1989b). *A Survey of Support Services for Special Educational Needs: Report by Her Majesty's Inspectorate.* London: HMSO.

GREAT BRITAIN. DEPARTMENT OF EDUCATION AND SCIENCE (1990). Draft Circular: *Staffing for Pupils with Special Educational Needs*. London: HMSO.

GREAT BRITAIN. MINISTRY OF EDUCATION (1944). *Education Act*. London: HMSO.

GROSS, H. and GIPPS, C. (1987). *Supporting Warnock's Eighteen Per Cent*. Lewes: Falmer Press.

HEDDERLEY, R. and JENNINGS, K. (1987). *Extending and Developing Portage*. Windsor: NFER-NELSON.

HEGARTY, S. and MOSES, D. (Eds) (1988). *Developing Expertise: INSET for Special Educational Needs*. Windsor: NFER-NELSON.

HEGARTY, S., POCKLINGTON, K. and LUCAS, D. (1981). *Educating Pupils with Special Needs in the Ordinary School*. Windsor: NFER-NELSON.

HELLIER, C. (1988). 'Integration – a need for positive experience', *Educational Psychology in Practice*, 4, 75–9.

HODGSON, A. CLUNIES-ROSS, L. and HEGARTY, S. (1984). *Learning Together: Teaching Pupils with Special Educational Needs in the Ordinary School*. Windsor: NFER-NELSON.

HODGSON, F. and TROTTER, A. (1989). In-service education and special needs. In: JONES, N. and SOUTHGATE, T. (Eds) *The Management of Special Needs in Ordinary Schools*. Lewes: Falmer Press.

HORNE, M.D. (1983). 'Attitude of elementary classroom teachers toward mainstream', *The Exceptional Child*, 30, 93–8.

HOUSE OF COMMONS (1987). Third Report from the Education, Science and Arts Committee: *Special Educational Needs: Implementation of the Education Act 1981*. London: HMSO.

INNER LONDON EDUCATION AUTHORITY (1985). The Fish Report. *Educational Opportunities for All?* London: Inner London Education Authority.

KIRK, S.A. and KIRK, W.D. (1971). *Psycholinguistic Learning Disabilities: Diagnosis and Remediation*. Illinois: University of Illinois Press.

LAWTON, D. (1988). Ideologies of education. In: LAWTON, D. and CHITTY, C. (Eds) *The National Curriculum*, Bedford Way Papers No. 33. London: Institute of Education.

LAWTON, D. (1989). *Education, Culture and the National Curriculum*, London: Hodder and Stoughton.

LINDSAY, G. (1979). The early identification of learning difficulties and the monitoring of children's progress. Unpublished PhD thesis, University of Birmingham.

LINDSAY, G. (1981). *The Infant Rating Scale*. Sevenoaks: Hodder and Stoughton.

LINDSAY, G. (1984). *Screening for Children with Special Needs*. London: Croom Helm.

LINDSAY, G. (1985). Introduction. In: LINDSAY, G. (Ed.) *Integration: Practice, Possibilities and Pitfalls.* Special issue of *Educational and Child Psychology*, 2, 3.

LINDSAY, G. (1988). 'Early identification of learning difficulties: screening and beyond', *School Psychology International*, 9, 61–8.

LINDSAY, G. (1989). 'Evaluating integration', *Educational Psychology in Practice*, 5, 7–16.

LINDSAY, G. (1990). Cognitive assessment. In: BEECH, J. and HARDING, L. (Eds) *Educational Assessment.* Windsor: NFER-NELSON.

LINDSAY, G. and DESFORGES, M. (1986). 'Integrated nurseries for children with special educational needs', *British Journal of Special Education*, 13, 63–6.

LINDSAY, G., QUAYLE, R., LEWIS, G. and JESSOP, C. (1990). *Special Educational Needs Review.* Sheffield: Local Educational Authority.

MILLS, K. (1988). Approaching an extended role for meeting special educational needs in high schools', *Support for Learning*, 3, 20–76.

MORTIMORE, P., SAMMONS, P., STOLL, L., LEWIS, D. and ECOB, R. (1988). *School Matters: The Junior Years.* London: Open Books.

MOSELY, D. (1974). *Special Provision for Reading.* Windsor: NFER.

MOSES, D., HEGARTY, S. and JOWETT, S. (1988). *Supporting Ordinary Schools – LEA Initiatives.* Windsor: NFER-NELSON.

MUNCEY, J. (1989). The special school as part of a whole authority approach. In: BAKER, D. and BOVAIR, K. (Eds) *Making the Special School Ordinary*, Volume 1. London: Falmer Press.

NATIONAL CURRICULUM COUNCIL (1989). *A Curriculum for All.* York: NCC.

NEALE, M. (1957). *The Neale Analysis of Reading Ability.* Basingstoke: Macmillan.

NEWELL, P. (1985). The Children's Legal Centre. In: LINDSAY, G. (Ed.) *Integration: Possibilities, Practice and Pitfalls.* Leicester: British Psychological Society.

NUTTALL, D. (1988). 'The implications of National Curriculum assessments', *Educational Psychology*, 4, 229–36.

ROBSON, A. (1986). The Welfare Assistant and the 1981 Education Act. Unpublished Advanced Diploma Dissertation, Cambridge Institute of Education.

ROBSON, A. (1990). Personal communication with the author.

RUTTER, M., TIZARD, J. and WHITMORE, K. (1970). *Education, Health and Behaviour.* London: Longman.

STEVENSON, J. (1984). 'Predictive value of speech and language screening', *Developmental Medicine and Child Neurology*, 26, 528–38.

SWANN, W. (1983). Curriculum principles for integration. In: BOOTH, T. and POTTS, P. (Eds) *Integrating Special Education.* Oxford: Blackwell.

SWANN, W. (1989). *Integration Statistics – LEAs Reveal Local Variations* (factsheet). London: Centre for Studies on Integration in Education.

SZADAY, C., PICKERING, D. and DUERDOTH, P. (1989). 'Special educational provisions – the classroom as a unit for analysis', *School Psychology International*, 10, 121–32.

TANSLEY, A.E. (1967). *Reading and Remedial Reading*. London: Routledge and Kegan Paul.

THOMAS, D. (1985). 'The determinants of teachers' attitudes to integrating the intellectually handicapped', *British Journal of Educational Psychology*, 55, 251–63.

TIZARD, B., BLATCHFORD, P., BURKE, F. and FARQUHAR, C. (1988). *Young Children in School in the Inner City*. London: Lawrence Erlbaum Associates.

WALLWORK, A. (1990). Support services for special educational needs in Bradford. Unpublished MPhil dissertation, University of Sheffield.

WARD, J. and CENTER, Y. (1987). 'Attitudes to integration of disabled children into regular classes: a factor analysis of functional characteristics', *British Journal of Educational Psychology*, 57, 221–4.

WEDELL, K. and LINDSAY, G. (1980). 'Early identification procedures: what have we learned?', *Remedial Education*, 15, 130–5.

WEDELL, K. (1985). 'Future directions for research on children's special educational needs', *British Journal of Special Education*, 12, 1, 22–6.

WIDLAKE, P. (1984). 'Beyond the sabre-toothed curriculum', *Remedial Education*, 19, 1, 13–20.

WIGLEY, V. (1989). *The implementation by teachers of skills learned on the EDY training course*. Unpublished MPhil thesis, CNAA. Huddersfield Polytechnic.

WOOD, J.M. (1989). *Mainstreaming: A Practical Approach for Teachers*. Columbus, OH: Merrill.

WOOLF, M. and BASSETT, S. (1989). 'How classroom assistants respond', *British Journal for Special Education*, 15, 62–4.

Subject Index

Author Index

...rway
NIGHT

STRIPES PUBLISHING
An imprint of Little Tiger Press
1 The Coda Centre, 189 Munster Road, London SW6 6AW

A paperback original
First published in Great Britain in 2015

ISBN: 978-1-84715-642-6

A CIP catalogue record for this book is available from the British Library.

Printed and bound in the UK.

2 4 6 8 10 9 7 5 3 1

ON A
Snowy
NIGHT

stripes

CONTENTS

THE FAR END
OF NOWHERE

Liss Norton

"He's there again," said Kaya to her little brother, Tuaq. The two Arctic foxes were playing and Kaya had just spotted the boy outside their den. He was crouched behind a bush, watching – just watching – the same as always. Kaya wasn't worried. The boy came most days and did no harm.

"Got you!" Tuaq yipped. He nipped the tip of Kaya's tail. Kaya rolled over, then sprang up and batted his ears. When she glanced round, she saw that the boy was laughing.

Summer slipped into autumn and the leaves turned sunset red. The wind blew cold. It whisked into the den, making Kaya and her family shiver.

Now when the boy came, he was wrapped up in thick layers. He blew into his hands and sometimes stood and stamped his feet. Occasionally he brought strips of meat. He threw them to Kaya and Tuaq and they gobbled them down, even though Mother had told them not to.

Mother said humans were dangerous. "They take Arctic foxes to the Far End of Nowhere and nobody ever comes back from that terrible place."

Kaya listened to her warnings, but the

boy didn't seem dangerous at all. How could someone who brought them food and laughed at their games be dangerous?

Winter came, bringing deep snow. Kaya's fur turned white and so did Mother's.

"Beautiful!" cried Kaya, twisting her head to admire her fluffy tail in the dim light of the den. Tuaq's fur was mostly white, too, but his ears were still the blue-grey of his summer coat.

The boy no longer came to watch. "I wish he'd come back," Kaya said, her tummy rumbling. "He brought good meat."

"It's too cold for him," said Mother. She was weary from long hours of hunting. It was getting harder to find little animals hiding underneath the snow for them to eat.

"Can I come hunting with you, Mother?" Kaya begged every day. She longed to learn all she could about catching food. One day soon she'd be grown up and have to fend for herself.

"No, Kaya," replied Mother, nudging her gently with her nose. "Stay close to the den and don't let Tuaq get too cold."

One day when Mother came in from hunting, a flurry of snowflakes whooshed into the den with her. "I daren't go out again," she said, even though she'd brought nothing to eat. "The wind's growing stronger by the second. There'll be a blizzard soon and I must stay home until it blows itself out. Humans send blizzards to blind the eyes of foxes so they end up at the Far End of Nowhere. That's not going to happen to me!"

"I'm hungry," whimpered Tuaq.

Kaya didn't say anything, but she was worried. Tuaq was too little to go for long without food.

"We have to be patient," Mother said. "I'll hunt again when the blizzard stops."

But it didn't stop. The next morning,

they could still hear the wind shrieking and the foxes huddled together in the den all day.

That night, Kaya lay awake listening to Tuaq whimpering in his sleep. She knew he was desperately hungry. Her tummy ached for food, too. She didn't know how much longer they could go without having something to eat, but Mother was too worn out from her long days of hunting to go into the storm.

"Don't worry, Tuaq," Kaya whispered. "I'll find food for us." She crept across the den and slipped into the tunnel leading out of their cosy home. The wind was still howling, but she didn't turn back. The thought of being outside alone at night was frightening, but she had to help her little brother. "I won't go far," she told herself. "Definitely not to the Far End of Nowhere."

The tunnel sloped up towards the outside world and the cold grew with every step Kaya took. Part of her wanted to run back to Mother and snuggle against her for warmth, but there'd be no food for Tuaq if she did that.

The tunnel opening was covered in snow. Kaya dug into it with her paws. It was deep and icy, but she kept on digging until at last her nose pushed through into the bitterly cold night. The whirling snow had turned the sky grey and she couldn't see the moon or stars.

As she scrambled out into the open, the wind flattened her thick fur and stung her face with snowflakes as sharp as stones.

"I'll break the ice on the river," she said, determined not to turn back. "And I'll catch Tuaq a fish." She wondered why Mother hadn't thought of doing that – the river was close to the den. If she ran all the way there and back she'd be home again before anyone noticed she'd gone.

Mustering all her courage, she set off towards the river, her paws crunching over the snow. She'd been there with Mother and Tuaq a hundred times. Surely she'd find it easily, even in a blizzard?

On and on she trudged, head down as she fought the fierce wind. "I'll be home in no time, just as soon as I've caught that fish," she said. But she walked a long way without reaching the river. "I must have gone too far," she said at last, feeling a stab of fear. "Maybe the snow's settled on the frozen water and I crossed without noticing it."

Forcing herself to stay calm, she turned and headed back the way she'd come, sniffing the air to find the fresh, clean river smell. But she could scent only snow, and its biting chill was tiring her out. "I'll go straight home," she said. "Even though I haven't caught a fish."

She lifted her head, trying to pick up her own trail so she could sniff her way back to the den, but the wind had blown that scent away, too. Heart pounding, she sped up, racing through the whirling snowflakes, desperate to find her home. But which was the right way?

On and on she ran until her legs ached so badly that she had to stop. Frightened, she threw back her head and howled. But the wind whipped her cry away and she knew nobody would hear.

Kaya tried not to think about the humans who sent the blinding blizzards, and the Arctic foxes who went to the Far End of Nowhere and never came back, but she couldn't help wondering if she was trapped in that terrible place right now.

She trudged through the snow, her legs as heavy as boulders.

At last she saw an enormous, dark shape ahead. She crept closer. Perhaps she could shelter behind it.

Kaya froze in her tracks – the dark shape must be a human-home! Mother had told her about their high walls that stretched up towards the sky. She shuddered, knowing now that the very worst had happened... She'd reached the Far End of Nowhere!

Too cold and weary to go back through the blizzard, Kaya spotted a low opening in a wall. She used the last of her strength to crawl inside for shelter.

When Kaya woke, the wind had died down. She remembered at once that she was at the Far End of Nowhere. Leaping up in panic, she looked around, her fur bristling with fear. There were no humans to be seen, just a heap of logs. Perhaps there was still time to escape! She ran to the hole she'd crept through last night, but before she could squeeze back out, footsteps came clumping towards her hiding place.

The footsteps stopped outside. Kaya crouched low, heart pounding and legs trembling. Did she have the strength to squeeze back through the hole and run to safety?

"Be brave, Kaya," she told herself. She dived out of the hole, past a pair of human feet in big boots. The human gasped. Kaya ran.

When she was far enough away to feel safe, she halted and glanced back. There were two human-homes here, the small one she'd sheltered in and a much bigger one that reached towards the sky, just as Mother had said. The human was standing between them. He was wrapped up against the cold, but Kaya recognized him at once. He was the boy who'd watched her and Tuaq playing outside their den.

Slowly, the boy inched closer while Kaya

stood, quivering, in the snow. He crouched down and spoke to her in his strange, human language. He held out his hand to her. She didn't move. Could she trust him?

The boy went into the big human-home. When he came out, he was carrying meat. It smelled delicious.

The boy threw a small piece of meat to her. Kaya's mouth began to water, but she picked it up carefully in her teeth. She'd carry it home to Tuaq. If she could find her way home...

The boy walked away from Kaya and threw down more pieces of meat.

Watching him closely, ready to run if he came towards her, Kaya crept forward. Now she knew there was more, Kaya swallowed the first piece of meat. She snatched up the next, before looking round for more. She'd save the rest for her little brother.

The boy was a good way off now, but he dropped more meat in the snow.

He wants me to follow him, Kaya thought. But why? She couldn't be sure, but he'd never tried to hurt her when he'd been watching near the den. Warily she crept after him, picking up the meat as she went.

Soon they were a long way from the human-homes at the Far End of Nowhere. Kaya was glad of that, though she wished she knew where the boy was heading. Suddenly her nose twitched and her eyes opened wide with joy. Home! She'd scented home!

As she darted forward, the boy smiled at her. He watched until she reached the den and began to dig down through the snow. Then he turned and hurried away.

Kaya dug frantically and soon uncovered the den's entrance. She dashed down the tunnel, woke Mother and Tuaq and set the meat in front of them.

"Food!" yipped Tuaq.

"Kaya, where did this come from?" asked Mother in astonishment.

"Let's eat first," Kaya said. "Then I'll tell you my story."

And what a story it was! She'd been all the way to the Far End of Nowhere and come safely home again.

Once they'd eaten Kaya snuggled down beside Mother, and Tuaq lay down, too.

Kaya gave a happy sigh. "On a snowy night…" she began.

HAROLD'S
ADVENTURE

Anna Wilson

Harold poked his head out of his hutch and gazed around Freddie's room.

"Oh! There's a nip in the air today." He shivered. "I'm going back to bed."

He withdrew into the snug warmth of his shell. Harold could feel a long winter's sleep coming on. Soon he was in that woozy state between being asleep and being awake. He was just thinking cosy thoughts about dandelion leaves when he heard:

"Will it snow for Christmas?"

Harold recognized the voice. It was Freddie. Harold could see him now, standing in the doorway talking to Mum. He hoped they were bringing breakfast.

"If it does snow, Harold won't get to see it," Freddie said.

"I don't think he would like snow," said Mum. "Have you got his box ready yet?" she went on. "It would be good to get him settled before the fireworks tonight. We always put him into hibernation on Bonfire Night, don't we?"

So it is *hiberation time!* Harold thought. *I knew it was getting colder.*

"Yes," said Freddie. "Here's the box."

Harold poked his head out a little way, watching as Freddie set his hibernation box down beside his hutch.

"I've got all the shredded paper and leaves and stuff. Look!"

"Well done," said Mum.

Harold drew back into his shell and smiled to himself as he listened to the comforting sounds of his cosy winter bedding being prepared.

"Mum?" Freddie said. "Why doesn't Boris hibernate?"

Mum laughed. "Because Boris is a cat! Cats don't hibernate."

No, thought Harold. *But they do spend*

most of their lives sleeping. Unless they're chasing me... That was another good reason to hibernate – a few months without Boris would certainly not go amiss.

The voices above him were becoming a background hum now as Harold drifted in and out of sleep.

At one point he had a vague sense of being lifted into the air, and wondered if perhaps he were flying. Then he yawned and nestled down. Tiredness had overcome him at last.

Harold dreamed of wandering through the garden in the sun, making dusty little beds under the rosebushes and nibbling at thistles...

"Oh, look at these! I didn't know we had
this many Christmas decorations!"

Harold blinked. The sun-soaked images
of the summer garden and the thistles faded
from his mind.

That was Freddie's mum's voice, he
thought. He opened his eyes slowly and
saw he was in pitch-darkness. *Could it be
spring already?* he wondered. *It must be if
I've woken up. But it's still so dark...*

The very thought of spring brought a
sleepy smile to Harold's lips.

Suddenly his box began to shake as if
someone was lifting it up.

"Oh my!" said Harold.

The bedding was slipping and sliding
around the box and he bounced up and
down.

I'm being taken outside! Harold thought.

He was excited. His mouth watered as he wondered what tasty treat he might be given to eat.

Thud! The box was set down.

Harold yawned and stretched. *This is it, then,* he told himself. *In a minute, Freddie will lift me out and I will be given a delicious salad leaf. Or maybe even a strawberry.*

He licked his lips, then he sat and waited as the sound of chattering voices floated above his head.

"Are we going to decorate the Christmas tree now? Please!"

That's Freddie, thought Harold. *What is he talking about?*

Harold slipped back into a doze, soothed by the familiar sound of Freddie chatting away.

"Oh, there's another box!" he heard Mum say a little later.

"I don't think there's room for any more decorations with all that tinsel…" said Freddie.

"I think you're right," said Mum. "Come on, let's go and hang the stockings up."

Freddie gave an excited squeak and then the voices drifted away.

I have no idea what they mean, Harold said. *I hope they come back soon*, he added, dozing off once more.

The house was very quiet now.

Harold peered hopefully up at the lid, wishing someone would open it.

"Freddie doesn't normally leave me this long," Harold said to himself. "Perhaps something has happened to him?"

A chink of light caught Harold's eye. The lid *was* open after all! Perhaps he should go and find Freddie himself. Maybe he was in the garden?

The lid of the box was quite high above

Harold's head, but luckily he was good at climbing. He had clambered up the shallow steps from the lawn to the patio more than once.

"Here we go," he muttered. He got a good grip on the side of the box and heaved himself up towards the light.

"Now, I'll just press with my front legs and my head," he said as he pushed against the side of the box. "And heeeeeaaave!"

He pushed and pushed with all his might, rocking back and forth on his hind feet as he did so.

Bump!

The box tipped over, the lid flipped off and Harold crawled out.

Carpet, thought Harold, as he sniffed the ground beneath his feet. He shivered. *It's a bit chilly for spring. And what are all these boxes? Perhaps there are other hibernating animals inside them.* He nosed at a cardboard box lying next to the one he had hibernated in. *This is most suspicious.*

He padded over the carpet towards the patio doors.

"Something's not right," he said aloud. "The light isn't golden and soft like sunlight normally is. It's silver and flat. I'm going to have to take a look outside."

Freddie often left the patio doors open so that Harold could wander in and out of the house. He decided to make his way over to them now. When he eventually got to the big glass doors, however, he found that they were shut.

"Oh dear," he said to himself. "If I can't

get out of these doors to find Freddie, I shall have to think of something else."

He stopped for a moment in a patch of silvery light and closed his eyes. "Come on, Harold," he muttered. "Think!"

Then he remembered that Boris had a special entrance to the house which he came in and out of, even when all the other doors were shut.

I've not tried it before, but if that lazy cat can manage it, I'm sure I can.

He made his way to the kitchen where Boris's door was. He looked at it for a moment, then he stood up on his hind legs and pushed with his front feet.

The flap opened rather more quickly than Harold had expected, and he found himself toppling forward.

He tucked his head inside his shell as he tumbled. "I hope I land the right way up," he said to himself. "Those stones will be hard…"

Harold *did* land the right way up, but the feeling under his feet was very strange indeed.

"I'm – I'm sinking!"

He panicked as his feet seemed to vanish before his eyes, disappearing under a white powder that covered the ground.

"And it's c-c-cold." He scrabbled with his claws, trying to find something to grip on to.

Finally his feet found solid ground somewhere beneath the soft silvery substance that glimmered and glittered in the strange light.

Harold caught his breath as he gazed around him. The garden looked so beautiful that he almost forgot how cold he was. The bushes and trees had been transformed into smooth white balls. He looked for the bird table – it was now silvery-white and gleaming in the strange light. Harold was amazed. Everything in the garden was covered in the same silvery white stuff.

What has happened? What is this?

Harold had never seen the garden look like this before. Where were the green leaves, the colourful flowers, the butterflies and birds? He thought about the bedtime stories he had heard when he was snuggled up at night in his box in Freddie's bedroom. There were many tales of witches and evil fairies casting spells on people.

Maybe someone has put a spell on the garden? he thought as he trundled around the lawn. It was hard work moving through the cold white stuff and he walked even more slowly than usual.

"I must find Freddie. But first, I need some breakfast to warm me up."

Harold searched and searched, but there was not a speck of green to be found. He felt he had been walking in circles for a long time and he was getting very cold indeed.

"Everything's changed," Harold said to himself. "The pond has vanished – there's only a slippery sheet of glass there now. And there are no birds. In fact, there are no animals at all – not even an earthworm."

Harold sat down and tucked his head and his feet into his shell to try and warm himself a little.

"What am I going to do?" He peeped out and looked up at a wall of white. "Where am I now?" He craned his neck to try to see better.

"Oh!" Harold stepped back in shock.

He was looking up at the face of a giant white animal. It had black shiny eyes and a mouth twisted into a smile. Its pointy orange nose quivered in the silvery light. What sort of an animal was this? Harold hoped it was friendly.

"I'm terribly sorry," said Harold. "I didn't see you. You must think I'm very rude. I hope I didn't tread on your toes." He took another step back.

The white animal said nothing. It merely looked down its nose at Harold, its eyes glinting. Harold noticed it was wearing something round its neck.

"That's Freddie's scarf," said Harold. "Hey! What have you done to Freddie?"

The white animal stayed silent.

"Oh, it's a secret, is it? Well, I don't like secrets and I don't like this white stuff and I want to f-f-f-find F-F-F-Freddie." Poor Harold really was shivering now. "I wish you would say something," he said. "In fact, I wish you would pick me up and take me back inside. I don't think I can climb back up through Boris's door. I am fr-fr-freezing... I'll snuggle up next to you, if you don't mind, and have a little rest. If Freddie comes to get his scarf, will you tell him I'm here?"

Still the white animal didn't move, but Harold thought his dark eyes glittered as though he understood.

Harold sighed and tucked his head into his shell. He huddled up against the large white animal and went to sleep.

Harold awoke to the sound of shouting. It was Freddie!

Thank goodness, he thought. *He's come to get me.*

He stretched one foot out – it didn't seem as cold as it had earlier.

He opened one eye. The silvery light had gone.

He opened his other eye.

I'm back in my hibernation box! he realized. *No wonder I'm not frozen any more!* He blinked and shuffled forward a bit.

At that moment, someone lifted the lid of the box and Harold was blinded by a bright light.

"Oh!" he squeaked and shot back inside his shell again.

"Look, Harold's awake!" he heard Freddie cry.

"I'm not surprised," said Mum. "We were making so much noise yesterday when we were decorating the tree. I can't believe I thought he was a box of decorations."

"Poor Harold. Have you been awake all night?" said Freddie.

Harold blinked as Freddie stroked his shell.

"Can I show him the snow?" Freddie asked his mum.

Snow? thought Harold. *Is* that *what the silvery white stuff is?*

"Quickly then!" said Mum. "It's not

springtime yet. We don't want him getting cold."

A pair of hands reached in and picked Harold up so that he came face to face with a grinning Freddie.

"Look." Freddie showed him the garden. "Snow – and on Christmas Day! It's so exciting! Happy Christmas, Harold!" and he gave him a pat on his shell.

Harold looked at the garden, still covered with white. It glinted and twinkled in the morning sunlight.

It does *look beautiful,* Harold thought. *Especially now that I'm not trying to walk around in it.* He gave a shiver as he remembered how cold it had been.

"Do you like my snowman?" Freddie said, pointing at the giant white animal, which was still wearing his scarf. "I bet you've never seen anything like it!"

Snowman? thought Harold. *So that's what you are.*

Harold nestled back in Freddie's arms and gazed at the snowman. How *had* he got back inside his box, he wondered? He wished he could ask the snowman, as he felt sure the creature would know.

The snowman looked right back at the little tortoise, and his dark, black button eye gave a slow, shiny wink.

"So it *was* you," Harold whispered. "Thank you, Mr Snowman. Thank you!"

SHE WHO DWELLS IN THE MOUNTAIN

Michael Broad

The herd of white woolly goats clip-clopped in the foothills under the shadow of the mountain. They huddled for warmth against the biting wind and munched on the last of the grass and shrubs. Winter was hard for mountain goats and the icy wind signalled a huge snowstorm was coming, which made them nervous. All except for one little kid. He was not put off by the cold, or the hunger, or the coming storm, and was hopping around his elders, pestering them with questions.

"When will I get my name?" he asked Proud-horn, the leader of the herd.

Proud-horn lifted his head up high, his fine horns jutting majestically for all to admire. "You cannot rush the naming," he said firmly. "I had to wait until my horns grew large and magnificent before my name was finally chosen."

"Who will decide what name I'll get?" the kid asked Wise-beard, who was the cleverest of all the goats and sure to know.

Wise-beard paused and wiggled his long white beard. "The herd have always chosen the name together," he said eventually. "And it is usually a name that reflects a goat's best qualities, most heroic deeds or truly magnificent features."

"Can't I pick my own name?" the kid asked Story-teller. She knew all the myths and legends of the mountain herds and told marvellous tales of brave goats with names like True-heart and Noble-hoof. "I want to be called Fearless-one!"

"I'm afraid you cannot choose your own name," smiled Story-teller. "Though there was once a little goat who tried to hurry things along. He ended up with a name he didn't like very much at all."

"What did they call him?" asked the kid.

"Doesn't-have-any-patience."

The kid burst out laughing and Proud-horn, Wise-beard and Story-teller chuckled, too, as they continued over the hard, frosty ground.

The goats could no longer find any food along the well-trodden path. The kid gazed further up the mountain where he could see many bushes and shrubs. Not only were there enough to eat, but also to shield them from the icy wind. The kid knew the elders didn't like to climb high in their search for food. He thought they were probably afraid of heights. Perhaps, if he was brave and went first, the herd would follow him.

Then they are sure to name me Fearless-one, he thought. With that, he clip-clopped away from the other goats, up the steep mountain edge.

The kid leaped from one narrow ledge to another. He was so sure-footed that he didn't feel scared at all. In fact, hopping all over the mountain came to him very naturally and it was great fun! He called down to the elders. "Come on up! Don't be scared – climbing high is easy."

The goats stared up at him, horrified.

"Come down from there this instant!" gasped Proud-horn.

"It's much too dangerous!" added Wise-beard, glancing around fearfully.

The little kid sighed, but he did as he was told. When he reached the herd the elders gathered around him and made a terrible fuss.

"What were you thinking?" demanded Story-teller, checking him all over.

"I wanted to find food and shelter… Also, I thought if I climbed up high you'd call me Fearless-one," confessed the kid. "And I think that would be a good name for me because I jumped on lots of the steep ledges and wasn't scared at all."

"We don't stay low because we are afraid of heights," said Proud-horn.

"Goats are built to roam all over the steep mountain ledges," added Wise-beard.

"Then why don't we climb higher?" the little kid frowned. "There's food and shelter up there."

"Because of She-who-dwells-in-the-mountain," explained Story-teller.

There was a hush in the herd at the mention of that name and everyone gathered round to hear the old familiar tale of how the woolly goats had been driven from the mountain.

"As your elders, we wanted to protect you, but it seems that now you are ready to hear the story. A long time ago on a dark winter evening, a herd of woolly mountain goats were clip-clopping across the mountain. They were enjoying all the shrubs they could eat when a sudden blizzard blew down from the frozen north. The goats quickly huddled together against the icy winds and ploughed through snowdrifts towards the caves high up on the mountain. But what they didn't know was that another creature was living in the caves…"

"Was it a mountain lion?" gasped the kid.

"Bigger than a mountain lion," replied Story-teller.

"A grizzly bear?" gasped the kid.

"Bigger even than a grizzly bear – and much more ferocious," she replied.

The little kid couldn't think of an animal bigger or more ferocious than a grizzly bear, so he kept quiet and let Story-teller continue with the tale.

"When the herd reached the high paths, they saw a bright orange light that guided them like a dazzling beacon through the darkness and blinding snow. The goats carried on through the roaring wind, hoping to find shelter, but what they saw on the path ahead was a red scaly dragon!

"The creature raised itself to its full height, until it was towering above them, and then it roared, blowing a ball of flame up into the air from its nostrils. Then the dragon snatched up some shrubs in her enormous talons and scorched the path right in front of them."

"Wow!" said the kid, his eyes wide with wonder.

"The herd beat a hasty retreat down the mountain and never dared to set hoof upon it again. We keep away from She-who-dwells-in-the-mountain and she keeps away from us."

"She-who-dwells-in-the-mountain is not a very good name for a fire-breathing dragon," said the kid. "It's really long and doesn't even mention the best bit, which is the fire-breathing."

"That is how she has always been known," said Proud-horn.

"How come I've never seen her?" asked the kid.

"None of us have ever seen her," replied Wise-beard. He looked up towards the mountain caves. "But we believe she's still there, so we stay down here where it's safe."

"I'm not scared," said the kid, still hoping someone might call him Fearless-one.

This was met with disapproving huffs and grunts from the elders, and then everyone fell silent. The wind had picked up, bringing snow down from the north, just like in the story. To make matters worse, the sun was already setting behind the mountain. The snow swirled on the whistling wind and the goats were soon covered in a white blanket that was growing thicker by the minute.

"We have to keep moving," yelled

Proud-horn. "This is the worst storm we've seen in years!"

"But there is nowhere to go," cried Wise-beard.

The kid thought about his short trip up the mountain. He hadn't seen any signs of a dragon. The elders obviously believed it, but if he could prove there was no dragon, he could lead everyone to the safety of the caves. *Then they will* definitely *name me Fearless-one,* he thought.

As the herd huddled tightly together, it was easy for the little kid to sneak away without being seen. He made his way up the mountain, hopping confidently. The blizzard battered the side of the mountain, but the woolly white goat was sure-footed on every ledge. When he finally made it to

the high paths, the tall shrubs and bushes
blocked the worst of the wind as he headed
for the caves.

The kid looked all about him for signs
of danger, but the path was deserted. Then
he heard the thunder of wings beating
overhead. The ground shook as an enormous
red dragon landed in front of him. The little
goat froze with fear as he peered up at the
great scaly beast.

"I don't want to be called Fearless-one any more," the kid whispered to himself.

She-who-dwells-in-the-mountain began to rip at the bushes with her talons and scorch the icy mountain path, just as she had done in the story. Too afraid to move, the kid squeezed his eyes shut and braced himself for a fiery blow. After a minute, the kid opened his eyes. Why hadn't the dragon attacked?

He watched carefully as she moved towards him – perhaps she didn't want to hurt him, after all! She was flapping her wings and pointing, as if she was trying to communicate. Then the dragon craned forward and took a long, deep breath, filling her lungs with air.

Suddenly Proud-horn, Wise-beard and Story-teller appeared out of the snow.

The stunned goats watched as the dragon filled the sky above the little kid with bright orange fire. But instead of running away, the kid wagged his tail.

"I thought he gave up on being called Fearless-one," said Proud-horn.

"He's going the right way to being named Foolish-one," added Wise-beard.

As the dragon made more flames, the little kid watched closely, and in the fiery patterns he saw pictures and symbols. He recognized the mountain and a shape that looked like a little goat. When he put them all together he could understand what the dragon was saying.

She-who-dwells-in-the-mountain explained that those who breathe fire can only speak in flames, but not to be afraid because she was trying to help them. The little kid was very relieved. He thanked the dragon and trotted back towards the elders.

"She's clearing the path to the caves so we can take shelter," he gasped excitedly, as the dragon continued to melt the ice. The kid watched as she picked up piles of branches and shrubs and carried them all up to the cave. "And it looks like she's gathering food and bedding for us so we'll be comfortable until the storm passes."

The dragon looked after the herd throughout the night. The goats learned all there was to know about She-who-dwells-in-the-mountain from the little kid and his amazing ability to understand the fiery language called dragon-speak.

The dragon told them how lonely she had been, and how she had once tried to make friends with a herd of goats in a snowstorm, but that they had all run away. Since that day, she had kept out of sight so as not to frighten them or anyone else.

They also learned that the dragon's true name was Fire-speaker, and when the elders gave their gentle host the honour of choosing the little kid's name, she wrote it across the night sky for everyone to see.

"What does it say?" the elders asked eagerly.

"Fire-listener," gasped the little goat, beaming in the orange light.

Fire-listener was very pleased with his new name — it was much better than Fearless-one.

STRIPY THE REINDEER

Katy Cannon

The evening air was chilly on the savannah.
Stripy the Zebra shivered a little as he
trotted along behind the herd. They'd
spent the day grazing and drinking at the
waterhole but now dark was falling fast and
it was time to head for open ground.

As the zebras reached their clearing,
Stripy's mother nudged him with her nose.
"You're on first watch tonight."

The rest of the herd settled down, a hush
falling over the clearing, and Stripy headed

off to keep a lookout. But his mind wasn't on keeping an eye out for lions. Instead he was thinking about adventure.

Stripy didn't mind standing watch. Every rustle in the grass, every shake of a branch could be a predator. If it was, he'd have to sound the alarm and save the day!

Except it was usually just the breeze blowing through the grass or the birds hopping in the trees. There wasn't anything to see except the very occasional cloud floating across the moon.

Stripy wished that just once, something *different* would happen.

He gazed up at the sky, picked a star, and made the same wish he made every night.

I wish I could have a real adventure.

Suddenly he spotted something. Something with *lights*.

Not the twinkling light of the stars he saw every night. These lights were getting brighter and growing closer. And they seemed to make a sort of ... jingling noise.

Stripy leaped up, ready to sound the alarm. But then he looked again – it didn't look like a predator. There weren't any teeth or claws, just a strange shimmer.

The lights grew closer still, until Stripy saw they were attached to a bright red thing. It looked a bit like the cars the humans toured the savannah in, but without a roof or wheels. The red thing wobbled and lurched in the sky, pulled forward by flying creatures Stripy had never seen before.

He gawped in amazement at the sight

of the creatures. They looked nothing like birds. Instead, they were shaped a bit like antelopes, except heavier, hairier and with huge antlers that stood proudly against the night sky. *Not* the sort of creature Stripy expected to see flying at all!

The red thing swayed to the side again before hitting the dusty ground with a bang as the animals landed. At the back, one of them groaned and fell over.

Stripy stared. The not-antelopes stared back.

A man jumped down from the flying car. Dressed all in red, with white fur round his neck and boots, he looked hot and bothered as he stamped round and kneeled down beside the still moaning not-antelope.

"Oh dear," he muttered. "Oh dear, oh dear, oh dear."

The other not-antelopes murmured among themselves, sounding very worried.

Stripy glanced behind him. The rest of his herd were all still peacefully asleep just a few metres away, unaware of their strange visitors.

"Um, hello?" Stripy said.

The lead not-antelope turned and

nodded his antlers in greeting. "Hello."

"What are you?" Stripy asked, very curious.

"We are reindeer, of course."

"Reindeer." Stripy tried the word out aloud.

"And not just any reindeer," the reindeer went on. "I am Dasher, this is Dancer. Behind us are Prancer and Vixen, then Comet, Cupid and Donner. And that one is Blitzen." He bent his antlers towards the reindeer lying on the ground.

"Is he OK?" Stripy asked. Blitzen lay on his side, whimpering, while the man stroked his fur.

"Too many carrots," Dasher explained. "The children leave them out for us, but most of us only eat a few. Blitzen ate every

77

carrot in Australia, and now he's ill."

Before Stripy could ask why children left out carrots, Dasher huffed. "The problem is, we're only halfway through our flight tonight – and we need all eight reindeer to make it on time."

"Make it to where?" Stripy asked, even though what he really wanted to know was how they flew.

"All around the world," Dasher said. "And all in one night."

"But … how?"

The reindeer smiled. "Magic."

Stripy looked at Blitzen's worried face, an idea forming in his mind. These reindeer needed help, that was clear. And he wanted an adventure… "The magic – is that what makes you fly?"

"Of course," Dasher scoffed. "Have you ever seen reindeer fly *without* magic?"

Stripy didn't mention that, until tonight, he'd never seen any reindeer at all.

"In that case … could the magic make another animal fly?"

"I suppose," Dasher said doubtfully. "But where would we find—"

"I could do it!" Stripy interrupted. "I could fly with you tonight!"

The man stood up and made his way towards them. "Well now, who do we have here?"

"A volunteer," Dasher said. "This… What are you, anyway?"

"I'm a zebra," Stripy explained.

"This zebra has offered to fly in Blitzen's place."

The worried crinkles on the man's forehead smoothed out and he smiled a wide, relieved smile. "A zebra who wants to be a reindeer, eh? That's exactly what we need! Do you think your herd would look after Blitzen until we return?"

Stripy glanced back at the other zebras. They wouldn't mind looking after Blitzen until he got back, would they? Not if they were helping a fellow animal in need, he decided. Stripy nodded, and the man beamed.

"Excellent!" He clapped his hands together. "In that case, I'd be honoured to have you pull my sleigh. But first you'll need a little of this..." Reaching into his pocket, he pulled out a handful of sparkling powder and sprinkled it all over Stripy's mane and back.

Stripy sneezed.

The man laughed, a huge belly laugh.

It didn't take long to get Blitzen settled in with the herd. Then, once Stripy had convinced his mum not to worry, the man harnessed an excited Stripy at the front of the sleigh, next to the reindeer called Donner. Behind them, Dasher grumbled about losing his place at the front.

Climbing back into his seat, the man took up the reins. "Ho! Dash away!" he called.

The savannah faded beneath them as Stripy flew up into the deep night sky, his heart thumping hard with excitement.

Air rushed past him, ruffling his coat, starlight shining on the white of his stripes. The gentle jingle of bells accompanied every stride as the reindeer (and one zebra) raced through the darkness.

Flying felt like swimming, Stripy thought, feeling the air ruffle his coat like water.

"This is amazing!" he called into the night, and Donner laughed beside him. "But where are we going?"

"Everywhere," Donner replied.

They landed on a city rooftop, lights

twinkling all around. Stripy stared as the man in red hopped out of his sleigh, grabbed a bag full of brightly coloured parcels, and disappeared down the chimney.

"Where is he going?" Stripy asked, fascinated.

"To deliver presents to the children," Donner explained.

In a flash, the man was back, tossing a few of the orange vegetables called "carrots" out to the reindeer. Remembering that they were what had made Blitzen sick, Stripy held back until Donner said, "Try one. They're good for you — as long as you don't eat a whole sackful!"

Stripy took a bite. It was crunchy! And it turned out that flying made a zebra very hungry.

Then they were flying again, stopping to deliver presents everywhere they went. They swooped down and landed on tiled roofs so the man could leave gifts for children asleep in houses, in mud huts with woven rugs hanging on the walls, in skyscrapers with huge, shining decorations, on farms … all without anyone spotting them. Soon they reached the edge of the land, with only water before them.

"Are we finished?" Stripy wasn't ready for the adventure to be over yet. Surely they couldn't have flown around the whole world already?

"Not even close!" Donner laughed.

They flew out over the wide, dark sea, across strange white mountains, and stone buildings tucked into valleys. Stripy tried to remember every sensation, every sight, to store away and think about during long nights on the savannah.

As they descended again, Stripy heard music from far below, near where a spiky-topped building jutted up into the sky.

"What's that music?" he asked. The air seemed to hum with the sound.

"Carol singing," Donner explained. "They're singing to celebrate Christmas. And look, can you see the lanterns they're holding?"

Stripy peered down and saw pinpricks of light against the darkness – like stars, but on the ground. "It's beautiful."

In each place they stopped, Donner told Stripy about how the people there celebrated Christmas.

"Some children leave out stockings," Donner explained. "Some leave shoes, or pillowcases, or even a suit of clothes for Father Christmas to fill the pockets! And lots of people decorate trees – some even decorate their whole houses. Look at that one!"

Stripy saw a house covered with lights, all flashing different colours – and on the roof, eight small reindeer made of white lights!

At one house, Stripy peeked through a window and saw two children tucked up in their beds. They'd made a sign that said "Santa, please stop here!" and stuck it to their door.

Stripy wished he could see the children's faces when they woke up and found their stockings full of brightly wrapped gifts. It was so exciting!

Finally, the man in red gave a whoop of delight. "My sack is empty! We've delivered every single present. Well done, my beauties!" He settled into his seat and picked up the reins. "Now, back to Africa to retrieve Blitzen, and let our brave zebra get some well-earned rest."

Stripy barely remembered the flight back across the ocean, the sky brightening as they flew. Before he knew it the sleigh was descending towards the familiar landscape of the savannah – and the sun was high in the sky!

The herd approached as they landed. Blitzen walked alongside them, looking much better. Climbing down from his sleigh, the man unharnessed Stripy, placed his hands on the zebra's back and grinned.

"Thank you, my friend. Tonight, you saved Christmas for millions of children. We couldn't have done it without you."

Stripy ducked his head, hoping Santa knew how proud he was to have been able to help.

In no time, Blitzen was back in his place and the sleigh was ready to leave. The reindeer all cheered Stripy then raced off, up into the sky.

"Anytime!" Stripy called after them, holding back a yawn. "See you next year!"

The herd surrounded Stripy, asking him question after question. Sleep could wait until he'd told them all about his big adventure – the story of the magical night when a zebra saved Christmas.

THE SPARKLE
PARTY

Tracey Corderoy

It was the day of the Sparkle Party and everyone in Snowdrop Wood was getting excited – especially Squirrel and his friends.

As they swept up the last of the dry autumn leaves, Squirrel was thinking. Every year, Badger, Hare and Mouse worked very hard, preparing the party for all the other woodland animals.

It would be so nice if someone did something for them in return, thought Squirrel. But how could Squirrel show them how much they meant to him…?

"Squirrel," squeaked Mouse. "Please could you help me move these plates over to the table? We can put cakes and biscuits on them later."

With that, a smile spread across Squirrel's face – stretching from whisker to whisker. Cake! Of course – that was it! To show his friends how much he appreciated them, Squirrel would make them a cake! They all loved cakes and Squirrel loved to bake…

But wait, thought Squirrel. *Would a cake be enough?* His friends did so much, after all.

He sighed and the tip of his fluffy tail drooped. A plain ordinary cake would never be enough to say thank you.

But who says it has to be plain, thought

Squirrel. *I could bake the most wonderful, most magnificent cake they've ever seen!*

Squirrel glanced at the clock. There were only a few hours left until the party. He needed to get started right away.

"I have to go home!" Squirrel cried.

His friends gathered round, looking worried.

"Are you feeling poorly?" Badger asked.

"No, no," called Squirrel, trotting through the snowdrops. "I just have to do something – now!" He waved goodbye and hurried straight back home.

When he got there, Squirrel took out his baking books to find the biggest, fanciest cake recipe. But as he flicked through the pages, he suddenly remembered – each of his friends liked a *different* cake.

Badger liked apple cake, Hare liked carrot cake, and Mouse liked strawberry cheesecake. Squirrel flicked through the pages of every book, searching for an Apple-Carrot-Cheesecake recipe, but he just couldn't find one anywhere.

"Oh dear," said Squirrel, closing his last book. What could he do now? But all of a sudden it came to him...

"I'll make *three* cakes," he said happily. "And build them into the most tremendous tower!"

The bottom cake would be an apple cake, the middle one could be carrot and finally the cake at the top of the tower would be yummy strawberry cheesecake!

Squirrel sketched out the cake. It would be tall and straight, with swirly icing as sparkly as snow. It would have sprinkles, and a big shiny cherry would sit right on the top. It would be the most amazing cake his friends had ever seen!

Next, Squirrel wrote down the ingredients he'd need. The list was *so* long, it stretched from his whiskers to his toes!

Now it was time to get started – there wasn't a minute to lose. Squirrel dashed around with his wheelbarrow, gathering up ingredients. Soon it was full to the brim with all sorts – flour, sugar, strawberries, eggs, butter, carrots and rosy apples!

Squirrel found three enormous bowls and bundled his ingredients in − sieving and whisking, cracking and stirring − with both paws *and* his tail! Normally, he would take his time and bake carefully, but today the clock was ticking!

As the cake mixtures turned from lumpy to smooth, Squirrel gave a satisfied nod. Who cared that the kitchen walls dripped with splats of egg. So far things were going tip-top!

Squirrel had just about finished his mixing, when all of a sudden…

Knock! Knock!

"Uh-oh," he gasped. "What if that's my friends? They mustn't see their surprise before it's ready!" Whipping off his apron,

Squirrel opened the door a crack.

"Hello," said Badger. "What are you up to?"

"Um, just … this and that." Squirrel replied, poking his head out a little.

"We've been missing you down in the wood," said Badger. "And we're about to hang the lanterns in the trees. Come and help us, Squirrel." He held up some pretty jam-jar lanterns.

Squirrel squeaked excitedly. He *loved* hanging the lanterns for the party!

But then he remembered – he had to *bake* the cake. Squirrel's whiskers drooped. "E-except," he spluttered. "I can't come right now because ... I'm a little busy."

Badger's smile faded. "But, Squirrel," he said, "the others are waiting for you."

"Oh…" said Squirrel. "It's just—"

He stopped and thought. Maybe he should tell his friends about the cake. They could hang up the lanterns and then bake it together after that!

But, if he told them, it would ruin the surprise. And it had to be a good surprise, too! Only a truly amazing cake would prove to his friends how much he appreciated them.

ON A
Snowy
NIGHT

"Sorry, Badger," said Squirrel. "I'll try to come later." Sighing, he closed the door. But staying at home would be worth it when he saw his friends' delight at getting their wonderful cake!

Back in the kitchen, Squirrel checked his recipe. The next step was to neatly spoon the cake mixture into three big cake tins. The problem was, he only had one tin.

Hare has lots of cake tins, thought Squirrel. While his friends were busy hanging lanterns in the wood, he could pop to Hare's house and borrow two tins. Picking up his basket, Squirrel trotted out.

Hare's house was in the middle of Snowdrop Wood, near where the party was to be. As Squirrel got close, he glimpsed his friends laughing as they hung the lanterns in the trees.

He longed to tiptoe over, scamper up a tree, then jump down crying, "Boo!"

But no – he needed to finish his cake. So Squirrel found the tins in Hare's cupboard and hurried home.

Back in his kitchen, he spooned the mixture into the tins, and popped the cakes into the oven to bake.

As they cooked, he started to clean up – sweeping, mopping and scrubbing. Poor Squirrel – there was ever so much to do!

He was *just* about to take the cakes out of the oven, when suddenly...

Knock! Knock!

"Oh no!" Squirrel panicked. What if one of his friends smelled the cakes baking? It would ruin the surprise!

Dashing off, he found his bedsocks and popped them on the floor just behind the front door. The strong whiff of these would hide any baking smell!

Squirrel opened the front door and stepped outside, where Hare was waiting on the path.

"Hello, Squirrel!" said Hare. "The lanterns are all hung up, so we're choosing the music now."

"Oooo, goody!" Squirrel clapped his paws in delight. Every year, he and his friends made up dances as they chose the songs – it was so much fun.

Bushy tail in the air, Squirrel trotted forward. But suddenly he stopped in his tracks.

The cakes – they were *still* in the oven!

"S-sorry, Hare!" gasped Squirrel. "I've

just remembered − I have to stay home a-and … wash my bedsocks!"

"Wash your bedsocks?" said Hare. "Couldn't you do that another day?"

"No!" squeaked Squirrel. "Have you smelled them, Hare? Poo!"

Hare's ears drooped. "It's starting to sound like your bedsocks are more important than your friends!"

"No, no!" flapped Squirrel, his tail all a-quiver. "I − just… Oooo!"

Squirrel couldn't think of anything to say. Then suddenly the smell of burning cakes wafted under his nose. He flew back in, shut the door and raced to the kitchen at once. But when he opened the oven door, a big puff of smoke billowed out.

Squirrel whipped out the cakes and gave

a great groan. "They've burned!"

Squirrel's big, round eyes now darted to the clock. There was no time to bake new cakes. The party would be starting in half an hour! Squirrel looked back at the sketch he'd drawn – perhaps if he piled the cakes up, his friends wouldn't notice the burnt bits!

Squirrel tried, but the tower would not stand up straight!

"Maybe if I *ice* it?" Squirrel wondered. "That might make it look a bit better…?"

Quickly he mixed up a *bucket* of icing. Then slopping the icing into a piping bag, he aimed it at the wonky cake. But *just* as he was about to squeeze...

Knock! Knock!

"Argh!" cried Squirrel. He jumped in shock and a giant squirt of icing shot out. It hit the cake and dribbled down messily.

"Oh no!" gasped Squirrel, dashing off to answer the door.

Mouse stood on the doorstep. "Hello," he said, smiling. "Come and blow up these balloons for the party!"

"But—"

"I've saved all the red ones for you!" Mouse said. Red balloons were Squirrel's favourite.

"I can't!" said Squirrel.

ON A
Snowy
NIGHT

"Why can't you?" frowned Mouse.
"What have you been *doing* all afternoon?
We've missed you!"

Squirrel shook his head. He'd missed
them, too. But he had to sort out the cake.
Now that his friends were upset with him,
it was more important than *ever* that their
cake looked magnificent!

"Mouse, I'm really sorry!" Squirrel said.
He shut the door and rushed back to the cake.
But no matter how many swirls and cherries
he added, it was just no good. It looked like a
wonky mountain splattered in snow.

Squirrel peeped through the window to
see a big silver moon rising in the sky. It was
getting dark. And that meant it was time
for the Sparkle Party. But what would his
friends *say* when they saw their surprise?

When Squirrel got to Snowdrop Wood, the party was in full swing. Crowds of animals played under the trees, and lanterns twinkled like jewels. There was lemonade, sandwiches and big cream cakes – much fancier than *his*! Squirrel looked again at the wonky tower and sighed.

"Squirrel!" beamed Badger as Squirrel plodded up. "What's that you've got – a cake?"

Hare and Mouse gathered round, too.

"So *that's* what you've been doing!"

Blushing, Squirrel hung his head in shame. He could hardly bear to give them the lumpy, sticky cake.

"It's for you," he murmured gloomily.

"To, um … show how much I care. It was meant to be *better* because I care a *lot*. You do so much for everyone else and I wanted to do something for you. But it didn't turn out quite right."

"Don't worry!" Hare patted Squirrel's arm. "You didn't need to make a *big, fancy* cake to show us how much you care."

"We know how much you love us *already*…" said Badger.

"Because *we* feel the same about *you!*" squeaked Mouse with a smile.

Squirrel looked at his friends and then he smiled, too. Now he knew – friends were friends, no matter what!

"Next year," he said, "let's make a *simple* cake together. That will be much more fun!"

With that, the music started and everyone skipped off to dance. And as they danced, it began to snow, covering everything in sparkly white. The snow was soft. The moon was bright. And it really was the most perfect night for a party...

THE CLEVER PUPPY

Linda Chapman

Minnie darted under the kitchen table and stared out at Katie with her bottom in the air and her tail wagging. It was far more fun being chased than being brushed!

Minnie was half spaniel and half poodle with a wavy golden coat, floppy ears and eyes the colour of milk chocolate. She was eight months old and she really didn't like being groomed.

"Oh, Minnie!" Katie said. She sat back on her heels and gave up. "OK, you win.

You can do without – just for tonight."

Katie put the brush down. Minnie immediately trotted out from under the table. She put her paws on Katie's lap and licked the tip of her nose. Katie giggled and pulled her in for a hug.

Minnie's tail wagged hard as she snuggled into Katie's arms.

Katie's mum put her head round the kitchen door. "Time to go, Katie."

Katie got to her feet. She and her mum were going to a Christmas Eve party in the village hall. There was going to be mulled wine, tea and mince pies for the grown-ups and hot chocolate and iced biscuits for the children. There was usually carol singing and games, too. Katie couldn't wait!

Minnie ran to the back door and whined.

She knew they were going out.

"Can Minnie come with us, Mum?" Katie asked hopefully.

"No, sweetie," said Mrs Young. "It'll be very busy and she might get scared with so many people about."

"But Minnie likes people," said Katie. "She wouldn't be scared, she'd love it."

"I don't think it's a good idea," Mrs Young said. "Come on, let's get our coats. It's cold outside."

Snow had been falling steadily all day and now there was a thick white blanket covering everything – the grass, the trees, the road. It was perfect timing for Christmas.

Katie quickly pulled a brush through her shoulder-length blonde hair and fetched her

her coat. When she came back into the kitchen, Minnie was still sitting hopefully by the door. She whined again.

"Sorry, Minnie, you can't come," Katie told her, going over and kissing her head. "But I'll be back soon. I promise!"

Minnie's ears drooped. She hated being left behind when Katie went out.

Katie and her mum walked out into the wintry world, the snow crunching beneath their wellies. The road outside Katie's house usually had lots of cars travelling along it but instead of the rumble of traffic noise, there was a peaceful silence. Up above them stars were just starting to twinkle in the dark sky. It all felt very Christmassy.

Katie turned to look at her house. Minnie was sitting on the back of the sofa looking out of the lounge window — she often perched there to watch people coming and going. Katie noticed something. "Mum, the lounge window's still a bit open." Her mum had opened it earlier so that the Christmas tree didn't get too warm and drop all its needles before Christmas Day.

"Oh, silly me! Can you just go and push it shut from this side for now?" her mum said. "I don't want us to be late!" Katie pushed the window shut from the outside. She blew a kiss to Minnie, who was pressing her nose to the glass and then followed her mum down the drive.

They walked through the snow, their breath freezing in white clouds. Katie turned back to look at their house one last time. "Mum!" she gasped. "Look!"

Minnie had managed to push the window open again with her nose and was now wriggling out through it. She paused on the windowsill then jumped down on to the ground.

"Oh no!" Mrs Young groaned as Minnie raced along the pavement towards them, her ears flapping as she bounced through the thick snow. She capered around them, woofing in delight. *Aren't I clever?* she seemed to be saying.

Mrs Young sighed. "You naughty dog," she said, giving Minnie's ears a rub. "We'll have to take you with us now or we'll be late for the party."

They set off again, turning on to the street where the hall was. Katie couldn't help smiling as the little dog bounded around her, leaving pawprints in the snow.

Suddenly Minnie stopped and cocked her head to one side. She whined and ran up to one of the houses lining the street, then she started scrabbling at the front door.

"Minnie, stop it!" Katie said. "Don't scratch Nancy's door like that!"

Nancy loved dogs but she'd told Katie she felt too old to have one of her own. She always came out to give Minnie a biscuit when she saw Katie taking her for a walk. Maybe Minnie was hoping for a biscuit now!

"Come on, silly," Katie said, pulling

Minnie away by her collar. "It's not biscuit time." But Minnie tugged her collar out of Katie's grip and ran back to the door. She started scratching at the door with her claws as if she wanted to get in.

Mrs Young walked up behind them. "What is Minnie doing?"

"I don't know!" Katie said.

"Minnie! Stop that!" Mrs Young said sharply.

Minnie paused, head on one side, listening. But as Mrs Young came towards her, she gave a bark and darted round the side of the house.

"Minnie! Come back!" called Katie anxiously. As she chased after her, Katie heard the clatter of Nancy's cat flap from the back of the house. "Mum! I think Minnie's gone inside!"

"Oh no," Mrs Young said. "I'd better see if Nancy's in." She rang on the doorbell but there was no reply. She opened the letterbox and called through. "Nancy, are you there?"

Woof, woof, woof! Katie heard Minnie barking from inside the house. She went to the window on the right of the front door and peered in. It was gloomy in the hallway but what she saw made her heart skip a beat. Nancy was lying on the floor at the bottom of the stairs. Minnie was licking her face. The old lady slowly sat up, looking dazed and upset.

"Mum!" Katie gasped. "Nancy's hurt! I think she might have fallen down the stairs!"

Everything seemed to happen very fast after that. Katie's mum called in again through the letterbox and Nancy managed to tell her that there was a spare key in the garden shed. Mrs Young found the key and she and Katie let themselves in. Minnie was sitting beside Nancy. She jumped up as soon as the door opened and raced over to them, bouncing around their legs. Mrs Young helped Nancy up and into the kitchen and then rang her friend Sue, who was a nurse. Sue was already at the hall for the Christmas Eve party so it didn't take her long to get to Nancy's house. She checked Nancy over but, apart from a few bruises and a twisted ankle, Nancy wasn't badly hurt.

"I feel so silly," Nancy told them all. "I missed a step as I was coming downstairs and must have fallen to the bottom. How did you know I was there?"

"It wasn't us, it was Minnie," said Mrs Young, shaking her head in disbelief.

"She was amazing," said Katie. "I tried to stop her scrabbling at your door, but she wouldn't – she kept on barking."

"I just thought she was being naughty when she wouldn't leave your door," said Mrs Young. She stroked Minnie's head. "I'm sorry, Minnie."

Minnie licked her hand as if to say, *That's OK.*

"She's a wonderful dog," said Nancy. She was sipping a cup of tea and a little colour had come back into her cheeks.

Katie glowed with pride.

"What do you want to do, Nancy?" Sue asked. "Would you like to stay here and rest or would you like to come to the hall?"

"I'd like to come to the party, I think," she said. "I'll be able to walk there if I use my walking stick."

They helped Nancy into her coat and found her walking stick, then they all set off to the hall together. Excited chatter drifted out through the open door.

They all went inside.

"Sorry we're late!" called Nancy as their friends gathered around. "I had a bit of a nasty fall, but this clever little puppy rescued me!"

People crowded around Katie, wanting to stroke Minnie and fuss over her. Minnie didn't seem to mind the crowds at all. In fact, she wagged her tail so hard Katie thought it might fall off! Lots of her school friends were there and they wanted to hear all about it.

"So, Minnie just ran up to the door and barked?" asked Jemima.

"How did she know Nancy had fallen over?" said Joseph.

"Mum thinks Minnie could smell that something was wrong," said Katie.

"And when you tried to stop her, she ran round and got in through the cat flap?" said Jemima. "She's such a cool dog!"

"She's awesome," her friend Ben agreed.

"She's the cleverest dog in the world," said Jemima, feeding Minnie a bit of her iced biscuit.

Minnie wagged her tail in delight.

"Carol-singing time!" one of the grown-ups called. "Gather round!"

Katie picked up Minnie and she and her friends went to stand in the circle with everyone else. Minnie snuggled as close as she could and licked Katie's neck as everyone began to sing *Oh, Little Town of Bethlehem.* Katie joined in, her heart swelling with joy. She was with her family and friends, it was Christmas tomorrow and she had the best puppy in the world. What could be better than that?

THE ONLY HOGLET

Jeanne Willis

Deep in the forest, in a den of dry leaves and sticks, a mother hedgehog lived with her one little hoglet. One baby wasn't many, but it was better than none and being the Only Hoglet made him all the more precious to her.

Like all hoglets, he was born bald and blind but his mother thought he was the most beautiful baby in the world. When he opened his tiny, bright eyes for the first time, he thought she was the most beautiful mother in the world. Being his Only Mother, she was all the more precious to him.

During the day, the Only Hoglet would curl up with his mother and sleep until the sun went down. During the night, she would leave him hidden under the blanket of leaves in the den, safe from swooping owls and fierce badgers, while she went off hunting for slugs and snails. Every morning, she came back and fed him until he was full.

The Only Hoglet grew nice and plump. He was no longer bald – he had thick brown fur on his tummy and his soft, baby spines had turned dark and prickly, just like his mother's. On warm evenings, she would take him out of the den and show him the best places to find worms and insects.

By the end of Autumn, the Only Hoglet was almost big enough to leave home. Almost, but not quite. He would have to be fatter to survive the Winter, and he still needed his mother to wash him and care for him and cuddle up with him while he slept. So the Only Hoglet stayed with his mother – warm, well fed and happy.

Then Winter came and everything changed. There was a sudden frost. It turned the mushrooms to mush. It nipped the flowers and blackened their petals. An icy wind blasted the last of the leaves from the trees and the river froze over.

One morning it began to snow. Bright, white flakes fell from the silvery sky and settled. Mother Hedgehog stayed in the den all day with her Only Hoglet and slept beside him, just as she always did. But on that cold, snowy night, she thought it best to leave him tucked up in his blanket of leaves while she went foraging for food in the frozen forest.

This time, there was none to be found.

The snow lay thickly on the ground. The mother hedgehog searched and searched, trying to sniff out slugs and snails with her long snout, but they were nowhere to be seen.

Mother Hedgehog didn't know it, but the fox was hungry, too. He came hunting in the shadows of the trees, but he could not find any mice or shrews to eat. Then, by the light of the moon, he saw her tracks and followed them.

The Only Hoglet waited all night long for his mother. He waited and waited. By the cold light of dawn, she still had not returned. He felt hungry and lonely and frightened.

134

The Only Hoglet waited until the sun had risen high above the trees, but there was no sign of his mother. By now he was missing her so much that he decided to do a brave but foolish thing – he crept out of the den and wandered off through the wilderness to look for her.

He had never been out of the den without his mother before. He had never seen Daytime before. Or Winter. As he shuffled through the snow, he saw icicles hanging from the oak trees and squirrels searching for long-lost acorns. But he could not see his mother anywhere.

He hurried through the trees, up to his chin in snow. He heard a robin singing on a bare branch and the distant sound of cows mooing. But he could not hear his mother.

He called for her, but she did not answer.

Finally, the Only Hoglet decided to turn back. But which way should he go? He was lost! He was hungry and tired and cold. All he wanted to do was curl up with his Only Mother.

Just as the Only Hoglet had given up all hope of finding her, he saw a rabbit with a fluffy winter coat disappear down a hole near the hedgerow. Maybe she would let him curl up with her in the warm, dry burrow and keep him safe. He dropped down the rabbit hole and scurried along the tunnel.

The rabbit was resting in a nest of fur. The Only Hoglet curled up next to her, but just as he was making himself comfortable, the rabbit felt his sharp spines in her side. She gave a startled squeak, thumped her feet and chased him out of the burrow.

The Only Hoglet hid under a holly bush, feeling sad. Other animals did not like prickles, it seemed.

The holly bush was covered in bright red berries and the ripest ones had already fallen on to the snow. Looking at the berries gave the Only Hoglet a brilliant idea! He lay down and rolled in them – round and round and round he rolled. When he stood up, he had hundreds of holly berries sticking to the end of his spines. He could not prickle anybody now!

On an island in the middle of the frozen river, a swan was sitting on her nest. The nest was lined with downy feathers – it looked like the perfect place for a cold, tired hoglet to sleep, so he skidded across the ice and slipped silently under the swan's wing. He had just settled down when the swan lifted a wing and spotted the berries. She was so hungry, she pecked them all off and swallowed them. The hoglet tried to snuggle up, but without the berries to blunt his spines, he prickled the swan. With a loud honk, she chased him from her nest.

The Only Hoglet slipped and slid back across the ice to the bank. He was exhausted, but he did not give up. He was determined to find some way of keeping warm, so he scuffled out of the forest and along the frozen furrows of a nearby field.

The stars came out. At the bottom of the hill, there was a farm. In the yard, a sheepdog was asleep in her kennel. Maybe she would cuddle him, if only he wasn't so prickly! The Only Hoglet curled himself up tight. He tumbled over and over down the hill until his spines were covered in several layers of fresh snow. He rolled right into the sheepdog's kennel like a snowball and came to rest in the straw under the sheepdog's chin. For a few blissful moments, he felt warm. But just as he was about to doze off, the heat from the sheepdog's breath melted all the snow off his spines and he prickled her on the nose. With a yelp, she woke and chased him out of the farmyard.

The hoglet ran back across the field.

The wind had picked up. It whistled and shrieked round a scarecrow standing in the ground and snatched away its woolly gloves. The left glove blew over the hedge but the right one went high into the air, spiralled down, down, down and landed at the hoglet's feet. He sniffed it carefully, thinking hard. If he crawled inside, it would cover his spines from top to tail. He couldn't prickle anyone like that! Carefully, he wriggled backwards into the glove and, with his head peeking through the cuff, struggled back up the hill to find someone to take care of him through the night.

The Only Hoglet reached the forest and began to run. But as he ran, the empty thumb of the glove fell over his eyes. He could not see where he was going. He ran blindly, here and there, and he didn't stop running until he bumped into a tree and almost knocked himself out.

High above his head, he could hear a squirrel chattering to herself from a hole inside the trunk. Maybe she would look after him! He began to climb the tree, hoping that she would wrap her fluffy tail round him and let him sleep in peace. But the glove got caught on a branch and, as he pulled, the wool began to unravel. Stitch by stitch, the knitting came undone. By the time the Only Hoglet had reached the hole in the tree, his spines were poking straight through the glove. When he snuggled up to the squirrel, he prickled her. She gave a screech which scared him and he fell right out of her drey.

The hoglet fell through the air and crashed straight into a wigwam of snowy sticks. As he landed, he felt something sharp and prickly and he squealed. Then he felt something shuffling and heard someone snuffling and his snout filled with the oh-so-familiar scent of home. He was back in his own den with his own mother!

She had not been eaten by the fox, after all. She had outwitted him and escaped, but by the time she arrived back at the den, the Only Hoglet had already gone. She had waited all day for him to come home. She had stayed awake and waited and worried. She had searched and called but when night-time came and he still hadn't returned, she had thought he was gone forever.

But here he was and here she was! So the mother hedgehog did what she always did. She fed her Only Hoglet. She cleaned him. She curled up with him and at last, he felt safe and warm. He fell fast asleep with his one and only mother and together, they hibernated for the rest of that long, snowy winter. And no amount of prickles could keep them apart.

THE MOON-GAZING HARE

Julia Green

"Bye, Dad! See you tomorrow!" Bea leaned over Granny's gate to watch the car reverse away up the steep hill. She waved and waved until the car had gone. For the first time ever, she was staying at Granny's house all by herself. But Dad would be back tomorrow, and he'd bring Mum and baby Ned, too, and it would be *almost* Christmas.

Bea went inside. She slipped off her shoes and lined them up next to Granny's boots in the hall. She ran into the sitting room to check all of her favourite things in Granny's house.

She found the wooden mouse in its usual place on the mantelpiece above the fire, picked it up and cupped it in her hand. She stroked its tiny nose with one finger. "Hello, mouse," she whispered in its perfect little ear. "It's me."

Granny came into the room. "All right, darling?"

"Yes!" Bea hugged her tight. Granny smelled lovely, like lavender and summer gardens. "I'm so happy to be here."

"I'm happy, too. We're going to have a very special time, just the two of us."

"The Christmas tree looks beautiful." Bea stood on tiptoe to reach a shiny blue bell made of glass, and shook it very gently.

The tinkling sound made her skin tingle. Two golden birds spun slowly in the wintry sunlight streaming through the window and at the top of the tree a star shone bright.

"Where's the train decoration?" Bea searched until she found it – a tiny wooden train pulling three carriages along a pine branch.

"That was Uncle Jesse's favourite when he was your age," Granny said. "And your dad loved the glass birds."

"Which is your favourite, Granny?"

"The silver trumpet. It belonged to *my* grandma, a long time ago!"

Bea smiled. She liked the way all the decorations had a story.

"I've been busy," Granny said. "Come into the kitchen and see what I've made."

Granny showed Bea the big tin with the Christmas cake inside, covered in white icing and decorated with a Father Christmas, a snowman and three fir trees dusted with snow. Everything was ready, waiting for Christmas.

So much waiting! It was too hard, having to wait day after day! Three more doors on the Advent calendar still to be opened…

"Would you like something to eat?" Granny asked. "Or a drink, Bea?"

"Not yet, thank you."

Bea slid in her socks over the shiny kitchen floor. She wanted to see everything in Granny's house first.

Granny laughed. "You're dancing with excitement!"

Bea ran upstairs, all the way to the attic bedroom where she would sleep.

The walls sloped in the shape of the roof. She pushed open the big window at the front and looked over lots of other roofs and chimney pots as far as the shining strip of silver that was the river. Today there was more silver than ever because of the floods in the water meadows.

Bea shivered and shut the window again.
She looked around the room.

Granny had put her old dolls' house on
the floor next to the bed, ready for Bea to
play with.

With both hands, Bea carefully picked up
the snow globe from the bookshelf. It was
made of glass and very heavy. She shook it
to make it snow. For a second everything
was a blur, until the white flakes settled
back over the little scene of fir trees, deer
and a tiny hare.

The hare!

She'd saved the best thing till last.

Bea shot back down the stairs, through
the kitchen and out of the back door into
the small yard, where Granny kept pots of
flowers and herbs, and a table and chairs

for warmer days. Between two big pots was the hare – Granny's moon-gazing hare, carved out of honey-coloured stone, its nose pointing skywards, its long ears smoothed against its back.

Bea kneeled down and ran her hand over the cold stone body of the hare. She pulled away the moss growing round its feet. "There, now you're free to run," she told the hare.

It was cold. The sky had cleared and later there would be stars. When the moon came out ... maybe, when no one was looking, something exciting would happen, like in Granny's story.

At last it was bedtime. After she'd drunk her hot chocolate and cleaned her teeth, Bea climbed into bed.

Granny tucked her in and sat down on the end of the bed.

Bea snuggled under the duvet. "Tell me your story about the hare, please, Granny."

Granny began. "A long time ago, a woman carved a magical moon-gazing hare out of honey-coloured stone—"

"Does it really happen?" Bea interrupted.

"Does what happen, Bea?"

"Does the stone hare come to life?"

"Well, that's how the story goes, as

you know," Granny said. "But the magic can only happen on very rare and special nights, when it's full moon at the winter solstice…"

"What's the winter solstice?"

"The shortest day and the longest night of the year. The twenty-first of December."

"That's tonight!"

"And there's a full moon, too. So tonight is extra-special. When the silvery moonbeams shine on the stone hare…"

Bea shivered with excitement. "The magic will happen," she whispered.

Granny nodded. "The hare will begin to warm up. She will twitch her nose, shake ars and stretch her legs. She will bound t of the yard, over the allotment across the fields, under the silvery light of the moon." Granny's words were soft like music. She sounded as if she was telling an old, old story. *Once upon a time…*

"Sweet dreams, darling Bea," Granny whispered as she tiptoed away.

Bea heard Granny turn on the radio and run a bath, and then, later, close her bedroom door. The old house creaked, as everything settled towards sleep.

But Bea was too excited to sleep.

She crept out of bed to the big window and looked out.

The sky was dark, but there were millions of glittering stars. Bea knew some of the names of the star patterns: the Plough, Orion the hunter, the North Star. As she watched, the moon rose. A big golden saucer, it climbed higher in the sky. It was so bright it made shadows over the rooftops.

It felt very late. Everywhere was quiet and still.

Bea pushed open the window and frosty air rushed in. She shut the window again fast. But the magic of the moonlight was too strong to resist. She pulled on her dressing gown over her pyjamas, put on her socks and slippers, and padded down the attic stairs, through the dark house to the kitchen.

Bea turned the key in the back door. She opened it and stepped outside into the yard.

Everything looked different in the moonlight. The bare branches of the trees made shapes like arms and fingers. Bea shivered. Even the bird table looked scary, like a tall figure standing very still and straight.

Be brave, Bea told herself.

The stone hare was holding its head up, gazing at the full moon. As the moon moved higher in the sky it began to shine on the hare. First on one ear, then its head, and now its whole body. The colour of the stone seemed to change to silvery-grey.

Bea looked up at the moon. She stared for so long her own eyes seemed to be full of the silver light. She turned back to the hare. Moonlight flooded the yard and bathed the hare with its silver magic.

Bea held her breath. Did she dare? She stretched out her hand to touch the hare.

She pulled it back quickly in surprise – the hare felt soft and faintly warm, quivering with life.

The hare stretched. It twitched its nose and waggled its long ears.

It sniffed the air and scratched at the moss.

Now it was exactly like a real, living, breathing wild hare.

The hare stared at Bea. Its eyes were large and silvery, reflecting the moonlight. It hopped forward, and looked back at her. It seemed to be asking her to follow.

Bea took one step then another but the hare didn't seem to be afraid. It ran ahead then stopped and waited for her to catch up. In a flash of movement, it was running again, out of the yard and across the allotment garden. Its paws left a dark trail through the frosty grass.

Bea ran after it.

The hare leaped and raced in big circles. It made Bea's heart dance to see it so wild and free. They ran together, playing chase, the hare always a little ahead. It was much faster than her, but the hare kept stopping to let her almost catch up, before it raced off again.

Bea laughed as they played together in the frosty garden under the moonlight. They raced between the rows of cabbages

and leeks. They played hide and seek behind the fruit bushes and the compost bins.

The hare stopped to nibble a spinach leaf.

Bea crept closer, until she was near enough to reach out and touch its silvery fur. This time, the hare did not run off. They sat together, the hare trembling slightly as Bea smoothed its back and stroked its silken ears.

"Thank you," Bea whispered.

And then the hare was off again. They ran and leaped and looped around the garden.

Bea stopped to catch her breath.

The hare raced on. It didn't look back. It didn't wait for her. It raced further and further away, over the fields.

Bea watched the hare until her eyes ached. She realized for the first time that her hands and face and toes were numb with cold.

The moon-gazing hare was so far away that she could barely make it out.

Could she still see it? Had it dashed into the woods beyond the fields?

She looked one last time for the racing hare, but it had disappeared completely.

Bea went back over the frosty garden, into the warm kitchen and locked the door. She crept through the house, all the way up the stairs.

Did Bea imagine it, or did the bell on the Christmas tree ring softly as she passed the sitting room? Was that the wooden mouse running along the mantelpiece? Was the snow in the snow globe settling over the tiny trees and deer, as if someone had just shaken it?

Bea climbed into bed and snuggled under the duvet.

She felt her toes tingle as they warmed up. She was *almost* asleep now. Happiness flooded through her. She'd seen the magic happen, just like in the story. She'd tell Granny in the morning. And Mum and Dad and baby Ned…

Outside, the moon-gazing hare ran on, through the woods and over the fields and in and out of Bea's dreams. One magical winter solstice night.

SNOWFLAKE
SURPRISES

Lucy Courtenay

It was Christmas Eve and the Christmas market outside the cathedral was closing up for the holidays. Figures in woollen hats whirled arm in arm on the ice rink that sprang up every year, while people bought last-minute biscuits, nuts and mince pies from the little wooden stalls ranged along the cathedral wall. Multicoloured light from the stained-glass windows dappled the cobbles and made the ice rink shine. The metallic taste of the air promised snow.

At the mouth of the mousehole beside the cathedral doors, Snowflake's nose twitched as she sniffed the warm, spicy smell of half a mince pie, lying forgotten on the icy ground nearby. She wished she was brave enough to scamper outside, but she'd never left the mousehole in her life.

Her big brother Nutshell puffed out his furry chest beside her.

"I'm going to get that pie for the Christmas show tonight," he said.

Snowflake lived with her mother, father and eight brothers and sisters: Nutshell, Blossom, Twinkle, Morsel, Trixie, Pixie, Pippin and Fiddler. Snowflake and her brothers and sisters admired Nutshell more than anything because he was big and very brave.

"But it's huge!" said Twinkle, staring at the pie. "You'll never be able to carry it, Nutshell."

"And the cathedral cat is always on the prowl at this time of the evening," added Blossom.

"Looking for food like us," added Morsel. He rubbed his fat tummy.

"I can run faster than that furball," Nutshell said.

Snowflake squashed herself against the earthy wall as her big brother darted outside. People stamped around him as he jumped this way and that. One false move and he would be squashed flat. Snowflake could hardly bear to watch.

Nutshell seized the broken mince pie and dragged it back to the mousehole, his tail whisking from side to side with the effort. His brothers and sisters crowded around as he tumbled into the hole with his prize.

"That was *so* cool!" Twinkle gasped.

Mother and Father Mouse appeared to see what the fuss was about.

"It's a beauty, Nutshell, dear," said Mother Mouse, admiring the pie. "But I wish you wouldn't take such risks with the cathedral cat."

"We'll put it in the middle of the table for the Christmas show," Father Mouse said. "Mince pies are Great-grandad Mouse's favourite."

Mother Mouse clapped her paws. "I can't wait to see you all performing tonight," she declared. "This year's show is going to be *wonderful*."

Snowflake felt sick. Last year, she had been too young to take part in the Mouse family's traditional Christmas show. Instead she had watched her brothers and sisters dancing and juggling and playing instruments, safely snuggled in her mother's paws. But this year was going to be different. This year, Great-grandad Mouse was coming and the show was going to be bigger and better than ever.

This year, everyone expected Snowflake to perform like her brothers and sisters – to make them gasp and clap.

Snowflake didn't know what she was going to do. She wasn't funny like Blossom, or musical like Fiddler. She certainly couldn't do anything dangerous or impressive like Nutshell. She couldn't sing, she couldn't dance. She couldn't do *anything*.

She felt her mother drop a kiss on her furry head.

"Don't look so worried, Snowflake. This evening is going to be fun."

Snowflake wished she could believe her.

Her brothers and sisters helped to carry the enormous half-pie deep into the nest. Snowflake stayed where she was. She looked outside again, taking in the colours, sounds and smells, the great glittering Christmas ice rink and the lights making patterns on the cathedral's stone walls. She wished she was as brave as her brother – Nutshell wouldn't think twice about performing in the Christmas show.

The Christmas table looked magnificent. Nutshell's half mince pie took pride of place. There were roasted chestnut crumbs from the chestnut stall and toasted marshmallow flakes from the marshmallow stall. There were breadcrumbs and raisins and even half a hot dog.

"I love Christmas time," said Morsel with a happy sigh.

The young mice sat down and tucked in,

talking and laughing, but Snowflake stayed by the door until Great-grandad Mouse had taken his seat beside the mince pie, then quietly slid into her chair.

Perhaps I can pretend I'm ill, she thought. Her tummy did feel a bit funny.

"What are you doing for the show, Blossom?" asked Twinkle, his mouth full of mince pie.

"Telling jokes," said Blossom. "What about you?"

"Armpit farts," said Twinkle. He demonstrated.

"I'm juggling raisins," said Morsel. "I was going to juggle five, but I ate two by mistake. So now I'm juggling three."

Snowflake nibbled on a piece of chestnut.

"What are you going to do, Snowflake?" Blossom asked.

Snowflake nibbled harder.

"I expect it's going to be a surprise," said Nutshell, smiling at her. "Isn't it, Snowflake? *I'm* doing something amazing."

Snowflake finished her chestnut crumb. She thought about asking for some of the great mince pie, but her appetite had gone.

"Show time!" Great-grandad Mouse said

as the table was cleared. He clapped his tiny wrinkled paws. "I'm sure you're all going to impress your old great-grandad."

The mice cheered with excitement and Father Mouse put another twig on the fire. Snowflake eyed the door and wondered if she could slip out without being noticed.

"Sit with me by the fire, Snowflake," said Blossom, putting a small paw on Snowflake's arm. "We'll get the best view of the show."

Snowflake found herself sitting by the fire with her big sister. She wanted to curl into a ball like a shiny brown woodlouse.

"Who would like to go first?" asked Father Mouse.

Blossom stood up and smoothed her fur. Snowflake's mouth felt dry. What was she going to do when it was her turn?

"What do mice put on Christmas cakes?" Blossom asked.

"Their teeth!" shouted Nutshell.

"Mouse-ipan!" Blossom beamed as she delivered the punchline.

The jokes got everyone in the mood for fun. Twinkle's armpit farts were loud and convincing. Morsel had eaten all of his raisins now, so juggled with three pebbles instead. Fiddler played on his matchbox violin. Pippin balanced on her head. Trixie and Pixie tied their tails together and did a double skipping act.

Soon, Nutshell and Snowflake were the only mice left to perform.

"Watch carefully as I escape from my own tail," Nutshell announced in a grand voice. "See how I have tied my hands behind my back just *so*. Prepare to be amazed!"

Snowflake couldn't imagine how her brother would ever break away from the complicated knots and loops he had made around himself. But with a spring and a leap and a roll that took him dangerously near the fire, Nutshell was free. He jumped on to the table and bowed to the loudest applause yet. Snowflake shrank back in her seat and tried to become invisible.

"What a magnificent Christmas show," said Mother Mouse with a sigh of contentment. "Well done, everyone."

Snowflake experienced a rush of hope. They'd forgotten about her! They—

"What about little Snowflake?" asked Great-grandad Mouse.

Everyone looked at Snowflake. Her

heart felt like a lemon pip, hard and sour in her chest.

"Have a try, Snowflake," encouraged Mother Mouse.

Snowflake shook her head. Her skin burned hot.

"A little song, perhaps?" said Father Mouse.

Snowflake wanted to please her family more than anything, but she had nothing to offer. Two tiny tears squeezed out of her black eyes. She wanted to vanish into the warm brown earth. With a little gasp, she whirled round and raced away from her family.

The mousehole glimmered at the end of the long earth corridor. The market stalls were empty and the cathedral lights were dark. Snowflake pelted outside. She felt cold gravel under her tiny pink toes, and freezing air whooshing into her lungs. She needed to get as far from the nest as she could.

Come and get me, cathedral cat, she thought as she ran. *I've let everyone down. I can't ever go home again.*

The gravel under her toes suddenly changed to something smooth and glassy. The sensation shocked some sense into her muddled head. She had run on to the ice rink.

The moon overhead made the ice glow like a great magic mirror. Snowflake stopped running but to her surprise, she found she was still moving. Gliding over the ice, she spun in a circle, slowed and stopped.

After a moment, Snowflake cautiously moved a paw. She slid to the left. She moved another paw and slid to the right. As she leaned to the side, she found herself making a gentle turn.

This was ... fun.

The ice flowed steadily beneath her in a white ribbon. Snowflake saw her tail flying along behind her like a streamer. She lifted her arms over her head and she felt beautiful and big and twice as brave as Nutshell.

Little white flakes began falling from

the sky. Holding out her front paws to catch the diamond shards, Snowflake spun and twirled as the snow danced around her. She felt as light as air, at one with the wind and the stars and the sky. When she heard small mouse paws clapping, she turned to see her whole family outside the mousehole, watching her.

"Great way to end the show, Snowflake!" Blossom shouted.

"You look as pretty as a piece of Christmas cake!" called Morsel.

"I bet I can skate, too," Nutshell said.

But the moment Nutshell stepped on to the rink, his paws shot off in different directions. His nose banged into the ice and he smacked himself in the mouth with his tail, before doing a forward roll and ending up on his back, staring up at the sky.

"Ow," he said, sounding dazed.

Snowflake helped her big brother back on to his feet. Then she skated away again, laughing.

"That little mouse is quite a surprise," said Great-grandad Mouse, nodding his old head. "Well done, Snowflake. Well done."

ANGEL DOG

Holly Webb

Penny looked at the Christmas tree and sighed. Dad had done his best to prop it back up, but it was definitely lopsided now.

"It'll look better once it's got some tinsel on it," her mum said encouragingly.

"Maybe if we put more baubles on one side it'll stand up straight." Simon sniggered, and Penny and Mum glared at him. "I wish I'd seen what happened. Was Candy trying to climb up it?"

"No," Penny replied. "A bird darted past the window, I think. You know what Candy's like – she'll chase anything. I did try to grab her, but she just launched herself across the room and crashed right into the Christmas tree. It's probably a good thing it was there, actually – she might have gone straight through the window if she hadn't hit the tree first." Penny shuddered. "She could have really hurt herself." She reached into the box of decorations for a string of silver tinsel then stopped short. "Oh no! Candy must have rolled on the decorations box as well, it's really squashed."

"Has she broken anything?" Mum hurried over to look in the box. "Oh dear, are the glass baubles smashed?"

Penny shook her head. "No. Just the decoration I made in school…" She held up the tattered paper angel. She'd only brought it home the day before. Penny had been really proud of the way hers had turned out, and she'd imagined it in a special place on the tree, surrounded by glittering tinsel and fairy lights. Candy must have landed right on top of it. The wings were torn and half the beads had fallen off.

"Oh, Penny. And it was so pretty. I'm really sorry. That naughty dog." Mum gave her a hug. "Put it up here on the bookshelf – we'll try and mend it later."

"She didn't mean to." Penny sighed. Candy never did mean to be naughty – but sometimes Penny wished they had a *sensible* dog.

Dad came in, blowing on his hands.

"I've shut Candy out in the garden for the minute. It's freezing out there, I wouldn't be surprised if it snowed. That would be an exciting start to the Christmas holidays, wouldn't it?" He eyed the tree. "Hmmm. It's got a bit of a lean, hasn't it? Oh well. We'll just have to try and keep Candy away from it. What are we putting on first? Lights or tinsel?"

"Lights first, Dad. We always do the lights first." Simon pulled them out of the box, and handed Penny one end of the string.

Penny loved decorating the tree. For her, it was the time Christmas properly started. As she wound the tinsel round and round, and found just the right place for each special decoration, she almost forgot her ruined angel.

Once Penny had attached the star to the very top of the tree, they all stepped back.

"Oh, that's beautiful," Mum breathed, as she flicked the lights on and turned round to look. It wasn't dark at all yet, but the twinkling lights made the tree seem magical all the same. "Lovely. I think we all need a mince pie and some hot chocolate!"

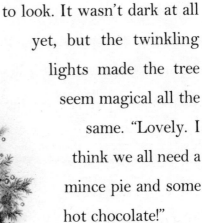

Mum and Dad disappeared into the kitchen, leaving Penny and Simon to admire the tree.

"What's that funny noise?" Simon asked, looking round the tree at Penny.

"What noise…? Oh!" Penny could hear it now, too – a weird, clanging thump coming from somewhere.

She frowned. "It's like – like somebody banging a gong…"

Penny raced out of the living room. The sound seemed to be coming from the back garden. She pulled open the back door. The cold air rushed in and she shivered. Somehow she just knew it was Candy, although she couldn't imagine how their bull terrier was making that noise. Bull terriers could be hard work sometimes, and today Candy was doing her best to prove it. She'd already crashed into the Christmas tree, squashed Penny's special angel, trodden muddy pawprints all over the kitchen floor and eaten six mince pies – and that was just in one morning.

"Candy!" Penny called, crossing her arms tightly. "Candy, where are you?" She stared out into the garden, feeling grumpy.

From round the corner of the house lumbered a strange shape – a white dog, weaving from side to side, with a metal watering can stuck on her head.

"Oh, Candy!" Penny forgot all about being annoyed. Candy looked so funny, wobbling along all confused. Penny hoped she wasn't hurt, but she didn't seem to be.

"How did you do that, you silly thing?" Penny asked.

Candy stopped and shook her head from side to side, as if to say she didn't know.

Penny giggled and rushed outside to help, forgetting all about the cold.

"Did you want a drink of water?" Penny giggled. "Candy, come here, let me pull it off." She could see that Candy could hear her – the metal spout was pointing at her now, and Candy shook it from side to side again.

"Look what she's done!" Penny said to Simon, who'd come to the door to see what was going on. "How are we going to get her out?" Penny asked, still giggling. "Candy, come here, good girl…"

"How did she get in there in the first place?" Simon wondered, shaking his head.

"You dim dog. I suppose it's because her head's so pointy. She can't get the can back over her ears. She could be permanently stuck!" He grinned, but Penny eyed Candy worriedly. She did look *very* stuck.

Candy pulled away from Penny and padded uncertainly towards the wall of the house. She swung her head so that the metal watering can banged against the stones with a deep, hollow clang. There was a huge dent in the side.

"Ow!" Penny put her hands over her ears to muffle the horrible clattering. "So that's what the noise was! But think what that sounds like inside the watering can! We've got to get her out of there, Simon – she'll hurt her poor ears. Candy…" Penny went over to Candy and crouched down, putting her arms round the dog's strong neck. "Don't worry, sweetness..." she said, taking hold of the watering can and giving it a tug. "Oh, wow, it's really stuck where she's squashed it." What if Simon was right, and she was stuck forever?

"It's all right, I was only joking," Simon said, when he saw his sister's worried face. "We can take her to the vet and get them to cut it off, if she's really wedged in." He smirked again. "Or the plumber, maybe..."

"Stop being mean and help me!" Penny told him.

Candy wriggled, whining miserably as they tugged at the watering can. She'd only wanted a drink – she'd smelled the water, and it had been so cool and fresh inside the can. She didn't understand why she was stuck. But now her ears were hurting.

Finally the watering can slid sideways and Candy was free. She stared up at them, her long white muzzle pink-tipped and foolish in the sunshine. She looked embarrassed for a second, and then shook her ears hard, as if she was checking they were still there. Then she gave a jaunty wag of her strong, thick tail and pranced off down the garden.

Penny looked doubtfully at Simon. "Do you think she'll be OK?"

Simon nodded. "She doesn't look very worried, does she?"

196

Penny glued on the last gold paper feather and looked down at her angel happily. Mum had found a stash of glitter and sequins, and the angel looked almost better than it had before Candy had landed on it.

"Do you like it?" she asked, leaning down under the table. Candy was collapsed on top of Penny's feet, nearly asleep. Penny didn't mind – Candy was like the best sort of hot-water bottle.

Candy looked up and sniffed eagerly at the angel. "No, I didn't mean you could eat it," Penny said sternly. "You've already squashed it once. And you have to promise to leave the tree alone."

At that, Candy padded over to the dog

bed. She flopped down and then shuffled around until she got comfy.

Penny peered at her. Her ears didn't look sore, but she was definitely worn out. It must have been scary, getting stuck.

"Poor baby…" Penny murmured. She looked thoughtfully at the sparkling angel, and then at the pile of craft paper. There was nothing to say her angel had to be *exactly* the same as before… She glanced over again, trying to see how Candy's ears went, then began to draw. Bull terriers were quite tricky – their long noses always looked a bit funny.

"That's almost right…" she said a few minutes later, picking up the scissors to cut out her paper dog. "You can fit just there. And I'll put some more glitter on as well…"

Penny tucked the paper Candy under one of the angel's golden wings and glued it in place. Then she sat back and admired her work – it looked just as if the angel was carrying the little dog.

Candy shifted in her sleep, yawned and snorted a little. Penny went over and scratched her behind the ears lovingly. "Silly dog. See, I've made you a guardian angel. Just in case you try jumping through any more windows."

The Life of an Arctic Fox

Clever and tough, Arctic foxes live in some of the coldest places on earth. These fascinating animals have found ways of surviving in very harsh conditions.

Family Life

Arctic fox families live together in underground dens. During the winter months, they dig burrows beneath the snow in order to get from place to place without going outside.

Staying Safe

Through the winter months, Arctic foxes have beautiful white coats – perfect for hiding from predators in a snowy landscape! When the snow melts and their Arctic homes become rocky, the foxes' fur changes to brown or grey.

Finding Food

Using their amazing hearing, Arctic foxes can locate the exact spot where their prey is hiding beneath the snow. To catch their food, Arctic foxes leap into the air and pounce, breaking the layer of snow and snatching up their prey.

Keeping Warm

Arctic foxes have thick fur on their paws, making it easy for them to walk long distances across snow or ice. They also use their fluffy tails like scarves!

KEY WORDS

Habitat: The natural home of an animal
Arctic: An area covering the far north of Europe, Russia and America

ARCTIC CIRCLE

Clever Creatures

From colour-changing fur to a long winter sleep, animals have lots of different ways of getting through the winter months.

Fly Away

As the weather gets chillier, lots of birds seek out warmer places with more food and shelter. Birds can fly thousands of miles in order to find the perfect spot to spend the winter months.

Thick Fur

Mountain goats grow an extra layer of woolly fur to keep them warm through the snowy weather. This coat will then fall off in time for the summer.

Eat Up

By eating lots of food through the autumn, animals can build up fat in their bodies, giving them energy for the colder weather. Some animals gather food in the summer and store it up – squirrels bury acorns so they have something to snack on in the winter.

Colour Change

In snowy habitats, animals often grow a white coat for the winter months. This helps them blend in with their icy surroundings, making them difficult for predators to spot.

Sleep Tight

Some animals, such as tortoises, hedgehogs and bears, spend winter in a deep sleep called hibernation. Their body temperature falls and they use up very little energy, meaning they can snooze right through until the spring!

THE
WINTER
WOLF

FROM BEST-SELLING AUTHOR
HOLLY WEBB

eBook available

THE
SNOW
BEAR

FROM BEST-SELLING AUTHOR
HOLLY WEBB

eBook availabl

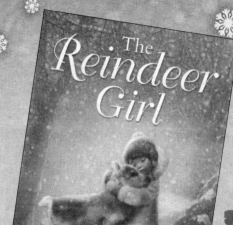

The Reindeer Girl

From best-selling author

Holly Webb

The Storm Leopards

FROM BEST-SELLING AUTHOR
HOLLY WEBB

ON A *Starry* NIGHT

An Enchanting Collection of Animal Tales

Moonlight
Tales

Heart-warming animal stories for sharing

WINTER
Wonderland
A Collection of Adorable Animal Stories

eBook available